G000230006

KENT COUNTRY CHURCHES
CONTINUED

An undiminished infatuation

Published by Meresborough Books, 17 Station Road, Rainham, Gillingham, Kent. ME8 7RS.

James Antony Syms first book of drawings, 'Kent Country Churches', has been reprinted by Meresborough Books at £4.50 (£4.95 by post).

Meresborough Books is a specialist publisher of books on Kent and a monthly magazine 'Bygone Kent', founded in 1979. Among over seventy books currently available is 'Exploring Kent Churches' by John E. Vigar at £3.95 (£4.35 by post). A full list of books and a sample copy of 'Bygone Kent' will be sent on request.

© Copyright 1987 James Antony Syms

ISBN 094819314X

Printed by Whitstable Litho Ltd, Whitstable, Kent.

KENT COUNTRY CHURCHES CONTINUED

An undiminished infatuation

By

James Antony Syms

MERESBOROUGH BOOKS
1987

CONTENTS
Churches Illustrated

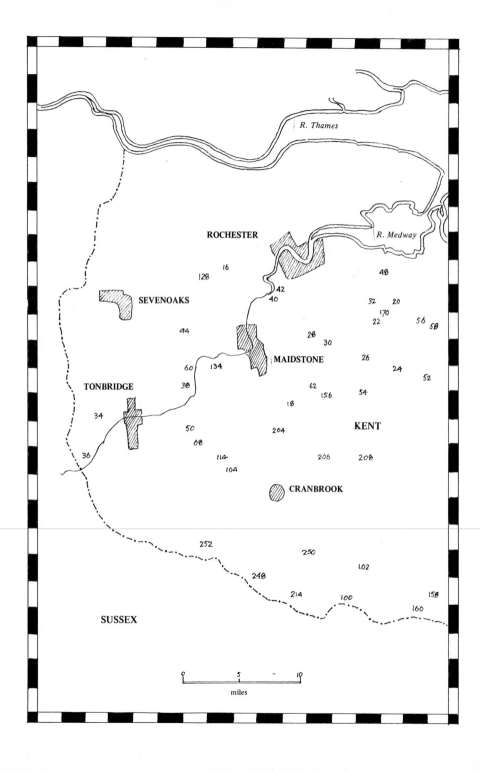

R. Thames

ROCHESTER

R. Medway

16
128

48

42
40

32   20
170
22   56   58

SEVENOAKS

94

28
30

26

24   52

60   134

MAIDSTONE

62
156   54

TONBRIDGE

38

18

34

50

204

KENT

36

68

114

206   208

104

CRANBROOK

252

250

248

102

214   100

158

160

SUSSEX

0   5   10

miles

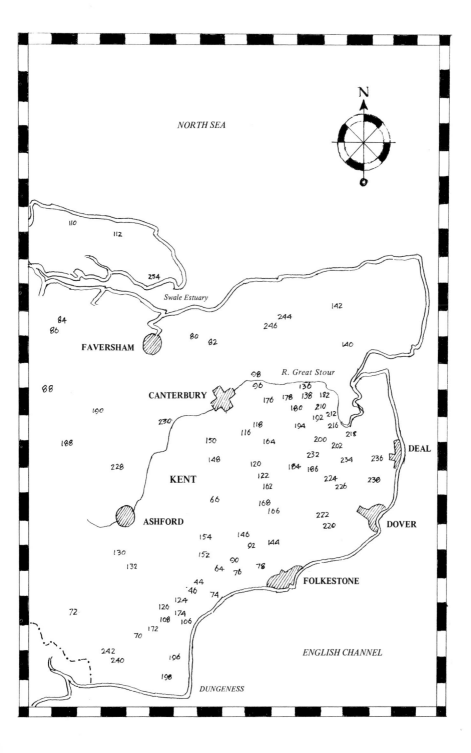

INTRODUCTION

This second collection of drawings of country churches continues my exploration of Kent and adds a further one hundred and twenty medieval churches to the one hundred and four described in my first book. On that occasion I concentrated on the village churches in the western half of the county simply because that is where I live; this volume restores the balance by emphasis on the eastern half. Each book is consequently somewhat unbalanced and, for a more complete picture of the county, both books are necessary. I must plead that the lop-sided make-up of each book was quite unintentional and due to geographical reasons rather than to any devious, subtle plan. To start with, I had no idea how many country churches there are; it has been an unlooked-for bonus to discover that there are so many. It makes one marvel at the depth of religious belief that must have existed in the first few centuries after the Conquest. I would think that the only building campaign of recent times that can possibly compare in magnitude but certainly not in quaiity is that of the railways. Let us hope the motorways never qualify.

Readers of this book may question why I have been to such pains to record, in an amateur and uninformed way, an aspect of the Kent countryside that is much more thoroughly and eruditely covered elsewhere. As I explained in my first book my reasons, briefly, are two: first to occupy the idle hours of retirement more fruitfully than, say, by knocking a golf ball fruitlessly round a golf course. The latter is a social exercise – mine is a solitary pursuit and probably better suits the less sociable, for the pleasures which one experiences from a solitary church can be diluted if shared too closely. My second motive was to provide some semi-permanent evidence of my existence and thereby to remind my descendants of one of their forbears who would otherwise vanish into oblivion. Regardless of its quality, a book or a painting can do that. A painting is better because, while a book can languish unopened on a bookshelf, a picture on a wall can hardly be ignored. Still, a book is better than nothing. For instance, I have in my possession a laborious tome written by that ancestor of mine who was vicar of neighbouring Barming. Although I rarely look at his literary effort, I am reminded by it of his one-time existence in a way that I otherwise should not be. So – two reasons for joining the already over-crowded bookshelves that seem entirely valid to me and which I hope will do so to my descendants.

I must also confess that I derive an unexpected enjoyment from both the sketching and the writing, so that these books are a form of harmless self-indulgence. Harmless, that is, provided one gives no unnecessary offence to any reader. I fear that, in this respect, I do, from time to time, allow my opinions to get the better of discretion. One particular prejudice that surfaces too often, I am afraid, concerns those churches, all too many, which one finds locked and barred. I accept that unguarded churches must be secure against the present scourge of vandalism and theft, but I cannot avoid the thought that locking the church is the easy way out and self-defeating at that. I am, in principle, in favour of the discouragement of crime and I suppose, regretfully, that it would be considered barbaric to bring back the stocks. Twenty-four hours between these wooden planks, anchored in a ghostly churchyard, particularly through the hours of darkness, might work wonders for the discouragement of future offences. I am also in favour of people accepting responsibility for their actions; convicted vandals should be made to repair, as far as they are able, the damage which they have caused. For centuries churches have been left open, day and night probably, and I expect that there were vagabonds as well as vandals to contend with in past society; there could be lessons to be learnt from medieval practice in dealing with the problem today. For instance, at Burmarsh on Romney Marsh, penitents were made to stand in the porch on a white sheet so that all who came to church might see — says the church pamphlet. I doubt if, as a punishment, that disgrace would have the same force today, but it is on the right lines, I think. Something must be done; churches should not be restricted to use on just one day a week and remain moribund for the other six. Too much of that and they will be moribund permanently. One may comfort oneself, though, that at least the buildings will persist even if largely inaccessible. Enough of this depressing hobby horse — I should hate to have my little book placed on some sort of modern version of the Index Librorum Prohibitorum or indeed to incur the wrath of the conscientious clergy.

In writing about any well-known subject, the newcomer is only too liable to expose his own ignorance and presumption. It is inescapable that I shall do that again in this book; it will, of course, be obvious that it is not written by someone qualified in architecture or ecclesiology and that my comments are founded on a conspicuous lack of educated knowledge buttressed by a growing element of prejudice — a character defect that appears to be a symptom of advancing age. My remarks, nevertheless, are based on a great interest in and affection for these old buildings which are such an adornment and feature of our countryside. I cannot now pass a medieval church without wanting to add it to my collection. It is as addictive as collecting antiques, but far less expensive. So my ignorance is mediated by enthusiasm and for that reason I feel able to hope for the patience and indulgence of the reader. If there is an absence of religious feeling in what I have to say, and one must admit that there is, I can only plead that others are better qualified than I to discuss this all-important aspect of our churches. Although on this subject discretion is the better part of valour so far as I am concerned, I must at least acknowledge that without an established religion we should not have the churches.

To come now, belatedly, to the choice of church in this book, my interest lies with the country parish church that dates from the medieval period in our history. I know that Victoriana has become more fashionable as that reign recedes, but I have not yet managed to develop a taste for its idiosyncrasies. Accordingly, Victorian churches are excluded but not Victorian restoration which cannot be avoided. Small churches are preferred to large churches, with or without their village, simplicity to ostentation, remoteness to accessibility and country to town. Kent is well endowed with churches that meet my preferred criteria and I am fortunate that this especial lode of magic is not to be rapidly exhausted.

When I first set out on my voyage of discovery in 1980, I knew precious little about the village churches in Kent, but when I saw them, I admired them. Now, six years later, I do know a bit more and my admiration has in no way diminished, rather the reverse. The architectural periods covered in my two books extend from traces of Saxon building to late Tudor. The Saxon and Norman styles are nominated as Romanesque by the pundits and the remainder as Gothic with the beginnings of Renaissance for the late Tudor. Romanesque architecture is identified by the semi-circular arch and by extravagant strength – at least that is how I claim to recognise it – and the Gothic by the pointed arch and economy of materials. The Gothic style, with which my chosen churches are mainly concerned, is sub-divided into:

Early English	1189-1280
Decorated	1280-1377
Perpendicular	1377-1500
Early Tudor (or late Perpendicular)	1501-1547*

The names by which these periods are known and their dates are included for the benefit of those who, like myself, find it difficult to remember the correct sequence of development and to relate the churches to the historical events with which they were contemporary. As a further aide-memoire for the historically forgetful the Angevins (Henry II, Richard I and John) coincided approximately with the Early English building, the Plantagenets with the Decorated, the Houses of Lancaster and York with the Perpendicular and, of course, the Tudors with the Tudor characteristics. Churches were built after the Tudor period, there is no denying, but it is the years from the arrival of Christianity in England to, say, 1600 that saw the extraordinary flowering of ecclesiastical architecture which delights us now. Apart from a nostalgic leaning towards the Romanesque, my own preferences are for the Perpendicular and Tudor styles – I will not attempt to define Perpendicular but one of its virtues, from my point of view, is that the vertical stone tracery of the windows is easier to reproduce on paper than the sweeping, flowing lines of the Decorated period. Lacking any technical qualification, I would hesitate to pontificate about the materials used in the construction of these churches beyond saying that I prefer the unrestored rubblestone or flint walls to the more recent, and no doubt more weather-proof, walls of geometrically knapped flint or the level courses of ashlared stone; a perverse preference, for the knapped flint and dressed stone will inevitably outlast the more primitive construction. Nevertherless, it is not altogether irrational to wish to concentrate my sketching activity on the older rather than on

* These dates are taken from Lawrence E. Jones' book 'The Beauty of English Churches'; others may vary the dating slightly. To avoid pedantry the dates should, of course, be taken as indications rather than hard and fast limits.

the more recent for fear that the former will disintegrate before the latter, as has happened to the mysterious Eastwell.

Bells, which invariably receive careful historical accounting in church leaflets, do not interest me, either as objects or by virtue of the music they make. I am grateful for their existence, nonetheless, for without them we would be deprived of the most striking feature in any church — the bell tower. It is the tower that seems to me to hold the whole structure together and it is undoubtedly the visual magnet that attracts one from afar. Despite a greater age, as a rule churches that do not possess a respectable tower never have the same appeal. It is a matter for congratulation that the medieval builders should have put so much effort and money into the building of a part of their churches that, one might assume, contributes relatively little to the religious element. As I try to remember when bothered by bell-ringing practice, without the bells we might be without the towers and they are certainly worth the clamour.

Churchyards, as the frame for a church, cannot be neglected when it comes to representation. What one hopes for on a first arrival is adequate space for a stand-off view with ancient yews or evergreens strategically placed to screen any surrounding eyesores but without completely obscuring the church and, equally important, a sufficient complement of mellowed tombstones to make an interesting foreground and provide an atmosphere of the past. The pleasure that one gets from old grey walls is inexplicable and, on the face of it, unreasonable. I think that we all experience this feeling to a degree and this book, like its predecessor, is just an expression of an attitude of mind that belongs to everyone of us. What I do not like, to list some of my more biased opinions, are shining new plate-glass cladding, modern tombstones, decorated with those hideous, green stone chips that do seem to be popular today, and the forlorn, unpruned, un-dead-headed rose bushes that occasionally line the path to the porch. Churchyards are the provinces of the past, epitomised by the ageing yews and old, tumbled tombstones; anything that requires attention and fails to receive it always looks misplaced and therefore well-intentioned efforts to brighten up a churchyard are never successful because the effort is so rarely maintained. Something like a yew, which looks better the older it becomes, is precisely what a church that follows the same pattern deserves. Generally that is what such churches get in the country, and that is why I so enjoy a solitary exploration of these places. It gives one a warm feeling of attachment to the countryside and one can sense the blood of past generations of Englishmen stirring in one's veins. It makes one look forward as well as back — to reflect on the generations yet to come who will, I trust, enjoy the same things and behave in a similar way a century or two hence. Future lives may be quite different but one common denominator could at least be the ancient stones that I have tried to depict in this book of drawings. As others have done too — but better. The critical might describe the foregoing as something of a purple patch but medieval churches are unique and marvellous and so unlikely to be repeated in today's material society that they merit much more than a patch of the purple — a paeon of praise on brazen trumpets would be the least they deserve.

Strangely enough it is the exterior fabric of the churches which, to my mind, is more compelling than the interior as a general rule. For most people the opposite is probably true, which may be why the grander memorials are to be found on the interior walls rather than in the churchyard; Churchill's at Bladon being a notable exception. Of all those inside, the memorials which I like best are those dignified dark grey slabs, ledger stones, which decorate the floors. Once, before the Victorians were let loose, the floors of all churches were, no doubt, paved with stone – cold they may have been but infinitely preferable to garish patterns of shining tiles or carpeted wooden floors. One is not meant to be comfortable in church, I suspect, so attempts to minister to the comfort of the congregation with heating and carpets is at the expense of atmosphere. Far better to worship in a beautiful setting and abbreviate the sermons if necessary; but who am I to pontificate who so rarely attends the services? Perhaps that is why I am so ready to condemn measures in aid of creature comfort in a place where the spirit should predominate.

A further argument in favour of the outside rather than the inside, for my purposes, is that the latter is immeasurably more difficult to draw satisfactorily; for one thing, one is too conspicuous when doing so and only the locally familiar can identify a church from an interior view. From the churchyard, on the other hand, the branches of an accommodating evergreen can always be drawn across the more intricate window tracery in the interests of simplicity without unduly violating reality; an invaluable strategem for an unreliable memory as well. Similarly a tombstone can be introduced to relieve a dull foreground without too great an extension of the artist's licence. One cannot, and should not, take such liberties with the interior except perhaps to add a helpful shadow.

One consistent absentee from my sketches is the human figure – for three reasons. First because people are extremely difficult to draw realistically, much too difficult for me; second because there is not often anyone present except myself anyway and, lastly, because it is the church that I wish to record, not the parishioner. With buildings as magically beautiful as these old churches, to limit my activities to the exterior of the church without human distraction is no hardship at all – not even in winter.

I have often wondered why these churches should exert so great a fascination. They do not compare in grandeur with, say, St. Paul's Cathedral or Westminster Abbey where, although impressed by sheer size, one does not feel the same identification with such national monuments. On the other hand, when one enters a simple country church one somehow feels at home; at least that is the effect they have on me. As one runs one's fingers over the ancient stones, as I invariably do, I must also confess to being soothed by their permanence and antiquity and by their apparent indifference to the changing world around them. Growing older I become, symptomatically for sure, more in sympathy with the past, which these venerable buildings represent, than with the immediate future, which they will outlast. Ancient stones are nostalgic; with advancing years comes increasing regret for opportunities neglected and one comes to suspect that one has let one's life slip by when more could have been made of it. Virtually indestructible, old stones correct that self-pitying indulgence; they are therapeutic and wholly benevolent in their effect on the onlooker, which must be another reason why they arouse so much respect and affection.

Preservation of these crumbling churches is a matter for the whole population and not just for the Church. There are commendable lay societies that assist where they can – and in Kent no book about churches should fail to pay a compliment to the Friends of Kent Churches. Another bouquet is due to the erudite John Newman who wrote the Kent sections of Pevsner's monumental 'The Buildings of England'. Without Mr Newman's two comprehensive volumes I should have had far more trouble in tracking down my subject churches and, having found them, would hardly have had a glimmer of what I was looking at. Pevsner has been my guide and tutor and I never venture out without him.

What does the future hold for all those simple village churches which have lost their congregations and now exist in tranquil obscurity? One reads only too frequently in local newspapers that this or that town church has been converted to a community centre, theatre workshop or even to use as a warehouse. Fortunately one cannot foresee such an undignified fate befalling the country churches – quiet redundancy with locked doors and protected windows seems more likely for many. If I was a member of the clergy the fate of these glorious buildings would haunt me and, if I could not persuade a congregation to attend, I would make it my business to be there myself as often as possible. To misquote Bishop Berkeley – 'When no-one is about, God is always present'. Alone in a solitary churchyard, what better company could one hope for? I am unable to resist ending my introduction with the famous pair of limericks provoked by the bishop's philosophy of the questionable existence of matter:–

'There was a young man who said, 'God
Must think it exceedingly odd
If He finds that this tree
Continues to be
When there's no one about in the quad.'
to which reply was made
'Dear Sir:
Your astonishment's odd:
I am always about in the quad.
And that's why the tree
Will continue to be,
Since observed by
    Yours faithfully
      GOD.'

For 'quad' substitute 'church' and one has, in lighthearted verse, a consoling and comforting outlook for the future of our country churches.

Hadlow, 1986

KENT COUNTRY CHURCHES
CONTINUED

RYARSH
St. Martin

Rye field

Ryarsh, an old favourite and near neighbour, opens the batting, so to speak, for this volume, the second innings of my sketches of Kent's country churches. Pity the poor selectors of any national sporting team; unlike them, in selecting my churches I have no problem of which to include and which to exclude — within my chosen field they all qualify and they bat consistently the whole way down the order. So here to receive the first ball, in midsummer 1984, is St. Martin at Ryarsh.

Separated from its hamlet by an outsize quarry and the M20 motorway, the church now leads a withdrawn existence, little disturbed by the passage of the seasons or, I would venture, by the demands of its scattered parish. I can imagine that it has probably always been thus for, although the churchyard has its full quota of listing and lichened gravestones, the interior of the church is bare of elaborate memorials — a few brass tablets to past vicars, that is all. As a matter of fact they do stretch in unbroken, recorded sequence for 750 years from 1231 and, as Arthur Mee observes, one of them founded the Kent Archaeological Society so perhaps I am being unfair to be so dismissive of the church's memorials. By any standards Ryarsh can be considered to have had a long innings and, if souls saved or people comforted are counted as runs, scored a few in the process.

There must have been earlier, unrecorded vicars, for the nave and chancel are Norman, witness the tiny Norman windows in each end and, as I thought, the traces of a Norman triplet of windows in the east wall of the chancel. Pevsner makes no mention of my 'discovery' so no doubt my detection was prompted more by hopeful imagination than by cold reality.

It is a very pleasant, modest, almost primitive little church variously known as Riesce in Domesday times, Riersce in 1100, Reyhersse and Ryersse in the 1250s, Rehersh and Reyershe in the 1270s, Ryersh in the 1600s and finally Ryarsh in the 1900s; so many different spellings to mark the lapse of time. I do not know whether rye is still cultivated in the surrounding farms, but certainly strawberries are and I was able to round off an afternoon's sketching in the hot sun by a little 'pick-your-own' in an adjoining field. The strawberries were delicious.

I suppose the church's most original feature must be that curious little tiled cap on top of the stair turret to the Perpendicular tower. I cannot remember many churches with a similar arrangement, but its near neighbour, Birling, has the same and possibly the one mason built both towers. At all events this capped turret gives the weathered old church a heightened and distinguished appearance with which to greet the visitor approaching through the open fields. The absence of a visible village, though, just a handsome farm and a pair of cottages, creates an atmosphere of placid redundancy after years of service and very likely redundancy is what the future has in store for Ryarsh. As someone who is retired from work I can confidently ask 'what's wrong with that?'. And answer myself — 'nothing when it allows one to sketch the countryside churches of Kent'.

CHART SUTTON
St. Michael

Rough common

Chart Sutton can never have been a place to provoke much comment although I do not know why not; Arthur Mee ignores it entirely and Pevsner gives it no more than a couple of cursory paragraphs. It is a straggling village with no discernible centre; if there is one it is definitely not provided by the church which is avoided by the modern housing. All that now remains in its lee is the village school and a large early Georgian house, to all appearances lifeless, but doubtless occupied, plus some handsome farm buildings. The welcome absence of activity (summer holidays) encouraged me to establish myself comfortably in the middle of the approach road, regardless of the highway code, and no traffic arrived to disturb my sedentary occupation.

While I sketched swifts wheeled and screamed around overhead. I do enjoy these acrobatic birds; in a curious way their excited cries create an atmosphere of nervous expectancy. Of course nothing ever happens as a result, but these summer visitors which fill the country air with their clamour never fail to raise one's spirits and expectations.

However, to get to the church – there was one here in 1080, but the present edifice dates from the 14th century. Only the tower survives from this great church-building era for the rest has gone, a victim like so many others of attack by lightning followed by fire. The replacement nave and chancel date from 1780 and 1890 respectively and no doubt that is why Pevsner and Arthur Mee could afford to disregard Chart Sutton. But viewing from the road, one can choose to be unaware of all but the medieval tower with its elaborately moulded doorway, the mounting block at the gate and the enclosing framework of trees.

A neighbour of ours at Hadlow once combined farming hereabouts with the duties of churchwarden. On one occasion, when digging a channel for a fresh water pipe to the vestry, he was startled to find that he had disturbed a communal burial place; the vicar was unworried and merely advised replacement of the bones and soil on completion of the work – presumably on the premise that the souls had departed and the bones were now simply so much calcium (or whatever bones consist of) to be disposed of without undue ceremony. In those days, say twenty years ago, Chart Sutton had its own vicar although, says my friend, the average Sunday congregation was less than double figures. One feels for the preacher; it cannot be easy to deliver a sermon to so few. Today Chart Sutton shares a vicar with the other two Suttons. Sutton Valence, the senior and central member of the triumvirate, is clearly visible from Chart Sutton's churchyard and I was tempted to position myself so that I could include the two churches in the one sketch – to try for a left and right so to speak. Hardly fair to Chart Sutton which can, in my opinion, perfectly well stand on its own merits without the help of its superior partner. In his conquering days Bishop Odo thought so too and he, if not entirely scrupulous in his dealings, was no mean judge of property in Kent.

BREDGAR
St. John the Baptist

Wedge shaped piece of land

Unobstructed by trees, Bredgar church stands in an open churchyard, roughly two to three acres in size, in the midst of its downland village. The present building was erected towards the end of the 14th century and is constructed almost entirely of flint. Use of this material has necessitated the stone reinforcement of all corners so producing a relieving ribbon of light to define the outline of the flint-dark church. The unbuttressed west tower is particularly well furnished in this respect by spectacularly substantial ragstone quoins. The tower is also remarkable for its west doorway, pure Norman with the characteristic zigzag mouldings; even I could identify the style without reference to Pevsner. It was apparently saved from an earlier construction and happily incorporated in the present Perpendicular building.

The building is a fine structure, as is only proper in a church to which was attached a chantry and a college in 1393; college is perhaps an exaggeration as I believe there were only a priest and three or four scholars there at a time. Now of course this old foundation only exists as a private house, but although its religious purpose has gone, the house still lends dignity and character to the village.

The church was firmly locked — double locked in fact. Secure in its spacious churchyard and closely overlooked, one would not have imagined that Bredgar offered much scope for undisturbed vandalism. I know that churches are vulnerable but somehow a locked church seems a denial of its function. If I might be permitted to ride my hobby horse for a moment, the thoughts that occurred to me, as I sat in Bredgar churchyard and wondered what the impressive east end concealed, may seem hopelessly impracticable, but they are well-intentioned nevertheless. For instance, most people are generally to be found at their place of work during working hours so why not the vicar? Could he not establish his office in his church, prepare his sermons there and so on so that everybody would know where they could expect to find him — including those with criminal intent. Naturally he would have to be away from time to time, but the mischievous could never rely on his absence. Multiple incumbencies create a slight complication, but one that could be resolved, to some extent, by rotation in the same way that the services are. Like most of us, the vicar must eventually retire from active duty; what more useful or appropriate retirement occupation than to act as a watch-keeping relief for the absent incumbent? At the end of the day the church would, of course, be locked but its hours of availability would have been greatly extended by the regular practice of using it as an ecclesiastical office as well as place of worship.

If I was a bishop, I think I might call on all my parish clergy to make proposals as to how the diocese should deal with this problem that currently seems to be solved by lock and key and that surely is not what the churches are there for.

Bredgar locked does not have the same message as Bredgar open.

What can one say about Hucking? To all outward appearances one finds a diminutive Victorian church, chapel almost, high on the North Downs, miles from anywhere and reached down lanes never designed for the motor car, let alone for farm machinery. Miles from anywhere it may be now, but might it not stand where the 'lost road' on the ridge of the Downs once ran — the prehistoric predecessor of the Pilgrims' Way below? As much might be inferred from Donald Maxwell's little book which traces the Pilgrims' Way from the borders of Kent in the west to Canterbury in the east. As an explanation for Hucking church being where it is that may sound unduly far-fetched, but it is a notion not easy to refute with hard facts and pleasant to entertain. No evidence for any early traffic remains. There are, it is true, a pair of cottages facing the churchyard gate and a farm immediately to the west; otherwise nothing but fields and belts of woodland. As can be seen from my sketch, the little church is heavily overshadowed by trees, but these, I imagine, are there more by accident than by design.

As one would expect, the church was locked, but in mint condition externally; the grass bordering the short path to the porch and along the verge of the lane had been mowed recently, the gate was operational, all the windows carefully protected by stout wire-mesh screens and, at the back, a small platform of steel scaffolding had evidently seen use lately. Someone is looking after Hucking church and it cannot be the congregation. Arthur Mee says that in Edward Hasted's day services were held once a month, weather permitting; in our godless age one could hardly expect the parson more often and in fact no services at all are held in the first quarter of the year. Why the seasonal discrimination, I wonder? But if there is no congregation and little in the way of services why the care and maintenance which seemed to me to be of a much higher standard than that enjoyed by many a more frequented church? Perhaps I was just lucky to find Hucking church in 1984; it is difficult to envisage a similar state of well-being in, say, fifty years' time. By then those sweeping branches and the writhing ivy that gave my pen such trouble are likely to have spread and undone much of the recent good work.

As to the church itself, it is an unassuming flint structure superimposed by the Victorians on a Norman base, a conclusion Pevsner draws from the simple rectangular plan. There is a pretty little bellcote at the western end of the roof and a chimney for heating just inside the porch; evidently they did not intend to be cold on those winter occasions when the parson came up from Hollingbourne.

It was a most pleasant experience to sit, undisturbed and unobserved (I think), on the edge of a ripening cornfield across the road to draw this curiously well preserved relic of the once religious life of the Kent countryside. I hope I have done justice to its state of preservation and of course to its air of mystery.

The church guide for Hollingbourne is so interesting that I am almost tempted to emulate its author and turn historian. One snippet of the past I cannot resist and will repeat; apparently in the years before the Conquest various villages were saddled with responsibility for the upkeep of the piers of the bridge over the Medway at Rochester – Hollingbourne's being the sixth. Why the non-riparian villages should have suffered this imposition is not related, but it would appear that the arm of rapacious bureaucracy had a long reach even in those days of limited mobility.

Hollingbourne is a choice spot on the Pilgrims' Way or the prehistoric track along the edge of the Downs, whichever tradition you prefer, and land has been held here by Aethelstan, son of King Ethelred 'the Unready', by the monks of Christ Church Priory, Canterbury and by members of the Culpeper family. It is the last named who have left the most distinctive impression on the church and make it so well worth coming to see and draw.

Dating from the 14th century, after damage was sustained through a violent earthquake (I have recorded many churches struck by lightning and damaged by fire – Hollingbourne is the first, but not the last, in my pilgrimage to have suffered from an earthquake) the church has experienced the usual additions and reconstructions and well-intentioned Victorian restoration. Now, in its spacious churchyard, presenting its north side and entrance to the Culpeper manor and village, it looks mellow and secure. I believe, and the guide supports this superstition, that the north side of churches was held to be the province of the devil which is one reason why the entrance porch and the major part of the churchyard of most churches are invariably on the south side; presumably with royal connections and the power of the Culpepers to call on, not to mention the prayers of the monks, the devil was not reckoned to have sufficient divisions at Hollingbourne, despite his attempt with the earthquake in 1382, to be an effective force and the superstition could safely be disregarded.

Externally, one's attention is attracted by the apparently windowless 17th century north chapel with its decorative band of faded black and white chequered triangles below the battlement. This is, or was, the sepulchre of the Culpepers and consists of a small, elevated chamber covering the family vault. The chapel seems to be built around a splendid central chest tomb, with marble effigy, to Lady Elizabeth Culpeper who died in 1638. She alone is memorialised here, but around the walls, arranged in orderly rows, are fixed blank shields on which it was doubtless intended to emblazon the arms of those interred in the sepulchre below. Only two of the many shields are so treated; heraldry, essential up to the Wars of the Roses, was no longer important when the chapel was built shortly before the outbreak of the Civil War. There are many other noteworthy aspects to Hollingbourne church, but none, I think, to match this display of Culpeper pride. How disappointing for its originator that the rapid march of events should have so completely frustrated his plans for his descendants.

THURNHAM
St. Mary the Virgin

Thorn bush settlement

Thurnham is one of the eleven medieval churches that punctuate the stretch of the Pilgrims' Way as it runs between the Medway and the Great Stour, a distance of roughly twenty miles, or one church every two to three miles. As staging posts for the pilgrims they do seem rather close together, but no doubt many of the penitents were halt and lame and hoping for a miracle cure at St. Thomas' shrine so a day's march of under five miles may well have been all some could manage. Next door to Hollingbourne, Thurnham now keeps itself demurely hidden from the passer-by. In this respect it resembles its worldly contemporary, Thurnham Castle, the remains of which brood, heavily overgrown and almost undetectable, on the rim of the Downs above. The church is well back from either of the two roads which meet here to form the geographical entity that is Thurnham, and is approached, unseen, down a leafy, enclosed and claustrophobic path.

Once the churchyard gate is reached, the prospect alters radically and one finds a substantial church set in the centre (more or less) of a large, open and immaculate lawn and fenced about by a low, unbroken, brick and flint wall. Fifty years ago Arthur Mee described this lawn as 'trim and well kept'; in 1984 I would go further and claim that the lawn would not disgrace Lord's cricket ground and that, if cleared of church, yews and tombstones, it would be ample for a full-sized football pitch. Appropriately enough, under this turf lies Alfred Mynn, the Victorian Kent cricketer. Someone must have cut the grass the day before I arrived for it had that shaven look that I strive for but never achieve in my garden.

The churchyard contained one novelty for me. Near the gate stands a headstone on which, by some technical process, two photographs are permanently displayed. They represent the deceased in old age. One might think this a desirable modern advance on an inscription, but the effect is not at all happy; to me it looks vulgar and I cannot really believe that the two people concerned would wish to be immortalised as they were in extreme old age.

The church was locked. It has a solid square tower, 14th century half the way up, Georgian above; I would not have noticed the four hundred year interval if Pevsner had not told me of it. There are blocked Saxon windows (so a church was here before Robert de Thurnham built his castle eight hundred years ago on the hill above) as well as Norman features and a north chapel which resembles the Culpeper chapel at Hollingbourne. As Thurnham's was added in 1603, Hollingbourne's must be the copy. The interior here should be interesting. Arthur Mee talks of a 'remarkable iron chest' and Pevsner of piscina, aumbry and sedile. He does not mention memorials despite the perpendicular north chapel which must have been added for some good commemorative reason, I imagine. It is always sad when a personal inspection is denied and I pray that today's despoilers are called to account if ever they do reach heaven, which I doubt. Come to think of it, it is a pity a few more doors were not locked in Cromwell's day.

St. Mary the Virgin and All Saints

There are three things that any observations about Boxley church must include; its idyllic village setting on the Pilgrims' Way, its western or galilee porch and its historical associations.

Setting first: Boxley, once the proud possessor of a 12th century abbey, now reduced to a simple parish church, lies in a belt of farmland below the wooded Downs. It is a minute village happily insulated from the urban spread of the county town by the M20. One must bless these motorways for their ability to restrain the expansion of metropolis into the surrounding countryside. The heart of this village is its rectangular green with the church dominating the east end and the King's Arms the west. Nothing in the least modern or industrial seems to spoil the prospect, although I should be surprised if Boxley does not harbour some small element of cottage industry; it is noticeable how many villages do and the practice appears to be spreading as the rates empty the towns.

Next the porch, or narthex as it is more properly called. This is the extension facing one at the foot of the tower in my sketch. I must defend myself here; the doorway and window are not mistakenly drawn off-centre — that is in fact how they are. This narthex, through which one enters the church, predates the main body as is clear from its traces of blocked Norman windows and doors whereas the rest of the church is 13th century or later. It would appear, so the experts say, that originally the narthex was the nave of an earlier church with the present tower substituted for the demolished chancel. It is contradictory, though, that the tower doorway, through which one passes to reach the replacement nave, should have all the appearances of a weather door with a drip stone arch as protection against the rain. Perhaps the parishioners originally intended to demolish the narthex too, but then changed their minds; it is said that it was used by the parish for business meetings and that seems as good an excuse as any for preserving such an interesting relic. I still wonder about that tower doorway, though.

Finally to the historical associations of Boxley. First chronologically are the Wyatts (spelt Wiatt in their memorial). The most famous, or infamous, Wyatt raised a Kentish rebellion against Queen Mary and suffered for his temerity with the loss of his head. Although I cannot find confirmation in my history books, my recollection of the memorial provides a second, earlier Wyatt victim of the axe. I could be wrong; these hanging memorials in the shadows of a church are often difficult to read. A more cheerful association is that with Tennyson who, it is claimed, used Boxley as the setting for some of his immortal verse. For instance, largely on the grounds that Tennyson once lived here and his sister is buried in the Lady Chapel, Arthur Mee suggests that the stream which runs through Boxley served as the model for Tennyson when he wrote 'The Brook'. Poetry does seem more appropriate to the felicities of the Boxley countryside than the unforgiving savagery of Tower Hill.

One of the column of Pilgrims' Way churches that leads below the Downs to Canterbury. Seen from one's car as one flashes briefly past on the Maidstone to Sittingbourne highway, it nestles unobtrusively and compactly against its wooded village. Nothing to get excited about really or to distract one's attention and certainly the authorities who wrote about Kent churches prior to Pevsner dismissed Detling with something approaching contempt. Pevsner is factual, but not particularly enthusiastic.

It is often agreeable, if generally mistaken, to disagree with experts, but I find Detling church charming. It is tiny, which I always like, mainly Early English with Norman traces and what the Victorians have added, the north aisle and the unnecessary broached steeple, do not offend here. Inside, there does not seem to have been must restoration; the stone-flagged floor remains undefiled by tiles, the pews are still boxed and the two piers that divide the nave and aisle are of that sturdy, unsophisticated square section that ensures stability and longevity. This interior is simplicity and honesty itself and I cannot imagine why anyone should want to decry it.

In monuments to past worthies it is lacking, but there are two objects which more than make good the deficiency. The first is a carved stone slab depicting a tonsured monk of the 14th century. The stone is much eroded apart from the features of the monk which remain virtually unblemished — miraculous, the credulous might have asserted in the past. The second and major piece is the slim, oak lectern, also said to be 14th century. It is silver grey, intricately and elegantly carved, and has that silky sheen of extremely old, polished wood that asks for a gentle caress. Its continued presence in Detling church is nothing short of miraculous.

Outside, the church is too set about with trees for a satisfactory rendering of its warm, old rubble walls and oddly structured roof and I was obliged to retire to the overflow graveyard across the road. The culprit, from a sketcher's point of view, is a widespread yew beside the churchyard path which looms over a pair of primitive, collapsing and crumbling chest tombs. I would like to have attempted these. The admirable Kent artist and writer, Donald Maxwell, must have been similarly frustrated by the difficulties of composition when he drew Detling for his much-reprinted illustrated walk along the Pilgrims' Way. In his case he concentrated on the tree-lined Way and on what he called 'Alpine Detling' to the exclusion of the church. Maybe he agreed with the experts.

St. Martin's is old and venerable although the small village is now mainly modern. Odo had it once, illegally, for he was forced by Archbishop Lanfranc to disgorge the manor to the See of Canterbury. Note that it was the manor they squabbled over, not the church. Even archbishops, to be fair, needed material sustenance as well as spiritual support and one can be sure that they got the former if not the latter.

STOCKBURY
St. Mary Magdalen

Swine pasture of the Stoke people

With advancing age I experience a mounting sense of frustration when confronted by a locked church. Stockbury was fuel to the flames. In unhappy contrast to unlocked and derided little Detling, the immediate predecessor in my progress, Stockbury is extolled by the experts and therefore one is all the more put out when one cannot enter to admire the much praised interior, let alone find any notice in the porch as to where the key might be obtained. There was an air of 'Leave me alone' about Stockbury's uncommunicative porch and I felt baffled. However, no-one likes to read a peevish tirade, so I will try to resist any further tendency to mention this painful subject.

To come, perforce, to the exterior of a building described by Pevsner as 'one of the most interesting Early English churches in the county', although sadly restored internally after a fire in 1836 it still presents a dignified appearance on the heights above the valley below. It is not modest; there is a Perpendicular west tower (displaying seven gargoyles and, more sinister, a vertical crack in the flint facade), three stair turrets, two transepts (one leaning perilously towards the south), two porches and two aisles. Not bad for a church threatened with redundancy and only saved, probably temporarily, by the agitation of its few parishioners.

The churchyard descends towards the valley and was mown and cared for. Indeed, as I drew, a young man was employed in measuring and deciphering the more legible headstones. He was doing this officially, so he said; presumably some form of local 'make-work' and I suppose no more futile than other such endeavours. He appeared happy with his occupation, as well he might in such a beautiful situation, but without any clear idea of its purpose. Nor had I as I sketched the tumbling tombstones beside the north transept.* Once before, when I attempted this church, I found a couple who make an annual pilgrimage from Cornwall to tend a parents' grave. It is a pity that crematoria seem to have displaced churchyards today – fewer people visit a crematorium, I fancy.

Unquestionably they chose a fine site on the crown of the Downs on which to place their church back in the 1200s. From it one can see to the north the far-off silver ribbon of the Medway estuary and the long, low hump of Sheppey; to the east, across the valley, great clouds of brown and orange smoke billowed – stubble burning – much criticised these days, but very dramatic it looked to me and a suitable subject for a painter like Constable I thought. To the south, immediately beyond the crumbling churchyard wall, lie undisturbed the grass-covered mounds of an iron-age fort now given over to apple trees and sheep. That leaves only the western approaches to account for; here is the church's sole visible neighbour, a farm plus, oddly alone in the adjacent paddock, a solitary, sentinel monkey-puzzle tree.

---

* A year later after visiting Bilsington on the edge of Romney Marsh, I could form a more respectful idea of why the young man was so employed.

LEIGH
St. Mary

St. Mary's church is arrestingly poised on an eminence above and dominating its village green; indeed while I was there, I was told that most sketches of the church were in fact undertaken from the green. Despite this well-meant advice and the visual attraction of the period cottages below the churchyard wall, I was not persuaded to relinquish my closer-range portrait from the lychgate. To be precise, it was the church I was after, not a work of art.

From where I sat, the church looked as if it had been standing four-square in its churchyard for centuries. It is supposed, in the church pamphlet, that there has been a church here for well over a thousand years, but, of the present building, most of the structure is surprisingly recent. Elements of this church, including the north wall of the nave, date from the 13th century; the base of the tower is 15th century and the not inconsiderable remainder a Victorian reconstruction. All this change is unusually well illustrated by some old pictures inside. The first of these chronologically is a drawing of what there was in 1797 – a squat, ungainly wooden tower, using as its plinth the bottom nine feet of the vanished 15th century stone tower, and a long, low-eaved barn of a nave roof with twin dormer windows. This drawing is corroborated by a watercolour said to have been exhibited at the Royal Academy in 1821 (entries cannot have been as fiercely contested then as they are today). However, improvement being deemed desirable, reconstruction was begun in 1860 so that by 1861 all that remained to be depicted were the 13th and 15th century stone arches and fragments of wall – no wooden tower and no nave. Extensive rebuilding has now resulted in a handsome gothic church of honey-coloured sandstone. An interesting relic of the past, though, that has been preserved, or revealed by the reconstruction, is a pillar of an earlier arcade presently enveloped in the north wall of the nave. One can still discern the coloured decoration on this survivor which makes one realise how colourful the walls of medieval churches must have been. I suspect that in their pristine state the effect would be considered garish today.

Leigh church does not boast anyone of historical consequence, but nevertheless there are memorials to attract one's attention. Inside the church, the central aisle is graced by a large ledger stone inscribed to 'Jesse Fitzer, citizen and saddler of London'. Having recently been given by my daughter a paper-back reprint of a book by Surtees, in my irreverent imagination Mr Fitzer seemed to spring straight from the pages of Jorrocks. Outside in the churchyard, a successful financier's memorial is gracefully flanked by arched lengths of wall in which there is provision for a chequer pattern of small wall plates for other deceased members of the parish. This seemed to me to combine respect for the departed financier with consideration for the less prominent parishioners and I was suitably impressed. Contemplation of memorials, compulsive though it may be, tends to over-concentrate one's mind on the past; as a compensating, if short-lived counter on behalf of contemporary activity, the porch was stocked with marrows, parsnips and other seasonable offerings in anticipation of the harvest festival. Clearly Leigh church is not just a mausoleum.

I should be very surprised if any inhabitant of, or visitor to, Penshurst agreed with me, but I find the village and church something of a disappointment. So far as I am concerned the reason is not far to seek – it is the tourist industry. It was a Monday in late September when I made my sketch and the visitors were not much in evidence, but I could sense the threat of them and the impact they must make on the village. In retaliation, the tourists would claim, with justification, that Penshurst is well worth coming to see. There is the beautiful 14th century palace, castle or manor (all three titles are appropriate) of Penshurst Place and there is the church closely bounded by Tudor brick walls and ancient, leaning, studded cottages; where there were gaps they have been sympathetically filled by the designs of George Devey, the ubiquitous Victorian architect in Kent, so that nothing clashes or is out of harmony with the church or Place. For all that, there is a slightly bogus air and, for someone who takes a pleasure in unrestored and crumbling ruins, Devey and the tourist blight have combined to erode some of the magic that an historic house like Penshurst Place must confer on its village.

As I say, few would agree with me and certainly the encircled church looks handsome enough. There has been a place of worship here since before the Conquest and vicars are listed from 1170, but the earliest surviving masonry, the round pillars separating the nave from the north aisle, is 14th century. The tower and the south aisle are 17th century and the Sidney chapel late Georgian. Leaving aside the latter for the moment, the outstanding feature of the church must be, I think, the small corner turrets, capped by pinnacles, that top the tower. They seem out of proportion and convey to me the imprint of Devey, but Pevsner says the tower is Perpendicular and the church pamphlet that it is early 17th century so unless the pinnacles were afterthoughts, which they might well be, I am wrong – as is often the case.

Now to the Sidney chapel. Here in the decorated Georgian successor to two earlier chambers are placed memorials that cover a span of almost seven hundred years. Mostly they commemorate the members of the one family, but the first, a worn, stone effigy of the upper half of a recumbent medieval knight, is joined by an uncle of Anne Boleyn as an involuntary guest of the family. The De L'Isles include one who lost his head in the reign of Charles II and a father-in-law, Field Marshal Lord Gort V.C. In the normal course of events he will be joined by his son-in-law, the present Lord De L'Isle, who also won the V.C. Such a double must make the Sidney Chapel and Penshurst church unique and gives it a distinction that would undoubtedly be appreciated by old Sir Stephen de Penchester, the warrior in armour.

My sketch, taken from outside the palisade of cottages, cannot include the south front of the church, but may perhaps illustrate to a degree what I have been complaining about.

EAST PECKHAM
St. Michael

East peak settlement

St. Michael's church is now in the care of the Redundant Churches Fund. To see it perched on the crest of a hill overlooking the wide sweep of the Medway plain and shadowed by towering beech trees, one cannot help wondering what sort of parish can ever have existed to justify quite so substantial a place of worship. There is no close-knit village – East Peckham itself is well away in the low ground with a new 'in-village' church – and St. Michael's only neighbours are the old rectory and Roydon Hall, both invisible. Here in the Elizabethan mansion lived the Twysden family, once famous in Kent affairs, but now entirely unrecorded in the local telephone directories which I find a reliable guide to contemporary presence or absence. Supporting evidence of the micro-size of the scattered parish comes from the list of the fallen in the last two world wars – five in the 1914-18 war and three in that of 1939-45, successive generations in one case, sad to say. So why a church here? Perhaps the Black Death cleared a hill-top settlement and left the church behind.

Nevertheless the church is not insignificant. My sketch shows the row of reconstructed Perpendicular windows, each carefully protected by a wire-mesh screen. What one cannot see so much of is the tower, now entirely covered by deteriorating stucco, and crowned with a slender, shingle cap. The tower stands directly on its footing, without benefit of a plinth, and is supported by no more than slim, clasping pilasters – all of which betokens considerable age. Pevsner does not date the structure precisely, but says that it was 'in the years before and after 1300 that it expanded to its present size'; no doubt from an earlier Norman base, vide a small Norman window in the north east corner of the chancel. He also relates the arches in the interior to the 1300s, but this assertion must be taken on trust (confidently, of course) as the church is securely locked. It used to be opened for a service once a year and once I was fortunate: my visit coincided with one of these occasions, though unfortunately it is too long ago to remember much.*

One of the first things I noticed this time was a crumpled piece of paper pinned to the churchyard gate informing one that the 'Weedkleen Service of Cambridgeshire' had recently sprayed weedkiller at the base of the walls. Good; the Redundant Churches Fund doing its stuff. But what this church stands more in need of is protection against the graffiti impulse of humanity. It is difficult to understand why anyone should wilfully despoil something with which they have only a passing, possibly never-to-be repeated, encounter and one wonders what must go on in the culprits' unpleasant minds and how the rest of their lives are conducted. I suppose that it is the collapse of belief in heavenly retribution which has released so many of our worst instincts today. I wish it could be otherwise – particularly for St. Michael's as it slumbers harmlessly amongst its beeches on the top of the hill.

* In June 1985, the Friends of Kent Churches held a symphony concert in the church; what nicer way to spend a Sunday afternoon and see the inside of a redundant church.

There are two St. Mary's at Burham. The one I have sketched is the medieval version, down by the Medway, and very much redundant once the village had moved away to the slope of the Downs. It is something of a rarity amongst redundant churches in that, although securely locked, one can see clearly inside through the ground-level windows. What one finds is a diminutive, white-washed nave and chancel of Norman plan. There are some painted wooden pews, the trace of a rood screen staircase, much evidence of small, blocked windows and the outline of an arcade that once gave on to a short-lived north aisle. It all looks clean and spare and altogether improved from the 'sorrowful wreck' described by Arthur Mee when he visited the church fifty years ago in the 1930s. Full marks to the Redundant Churches Trust.

In the neatly fenced churchyard I found a tethered goat grazing peacefully between the yews and headstones. I have only recently realised what gorgeous creatures goats can become with proper grooming, my enlightenment occurring at the 1984 Kent Agricultural Show at Detling. There I found that the impressive, elephantine bulls and the immaculate, barbered sheep couldn't begin to compare with the wise and patient faces of the goats in their long, luxurious, silken coats. So an elegant, omnivorous goat can only be an asset to any churchyard, even one that can no longer expect any addition to its quota of the faithful.

My sketch, undertaken between fitful gusts of rain and bursts of autumnal sunshine in the company of wheeling scavenging gulls, was made from below the embanked Medway where the river forms a great meandering horseshoe. Behind me, on the opposite bank, loomed a huge paper mill with what looked like piles of waste paper waiting to be pulped. It could not be a more unfortunate juxtaposition of the beautiful past and the ugly industrial present. In making this disapproving comparison, one conveniently forgets that, without modern industry, there would be no paper on which to print books like this. So much the better, some might say.

It was here, between Snodland and Burham, that Canterbury pilgrims are thought to have crossed the Medway and what more appropriate place to build a church. I dare say the river presented something of an obstacle in those days and prayers for its successful negotiation would not have been out of place. This historic stretch of the Medway is a sad come-down today — no pilgrims, an abandoned church and an overbearing, industrial presence — but one can predict with confidence that, when the mills have gone and unspoilt nature returns, the medieval church will still be standing to mark the vanished crossing, witness to a pre-industrial age when ignorance and religious faith combined miraculously to create enduring and enchanting structures. But will there then be pilgrims to admire the achievements of a more credulous age, one asks with less confidence?

I am ashamed to say that I always take a perverse pleasure when experts appear to contradict each other. Here at Wouldham the church is very old with Saxon origins and a 12th century, i.e. Norman aisle, says Pevsner. But that earlier cataloguer of ecclesiastical architecture in Kent, Sir Stephen Glynne, states firmly that the church exhibits 'every style except Norman'. Certainly the church was recorded in the Domesday Book which was compiled in 1086.

When one stands inside one is conscious of an excess of massive pillars defining the aisles from the nave. It is not a large building, quite the contrary, and the impression one gets is of columns crowding out the limited space available for the congregation. Evidently the medieval builders, or re-builders, were determined that, whatever else happened, the roof would remain supported and the church would not fall down. These medieval churches rarely do; they may be struck by lightning or be burnt by fire but their walls do tend to remain standing.

Of the Saxon settlement at Wouldham nothing remains, nor is there much evidence of anything prior to Victoria, apart from the church of course. One now sees a Victorian mining village running parallel to the Medway – about where the Roman invaders forded the river after trouble with the natives at Aylesford, suggests the erudite church booklet. Like all mining villages, Wouldham is no doubt full of character but rather drab in appearance. What is, or was, mined (or, more correctly, quarried) here is chalk from the Downs above, not coal, and in 1984 that is a mercy.

My view is the conventional one, I think. Beyond, to the west is the river separated only by an untidy strip of waste – not suitable for a portrait. The bonus, from my point of view, lies with one of the tombstones flanking the churchyard path. In historical terms, and apparently in the opinion of the village, this grave is held to be of comparable status to that of the church and I would not disagree. Here lies, as the recently recut inscription clearly states 'Walter Burke, purser on (sic) His Majesty's Ship Victory in the Glorious Battle of Trafalgar and in his Arms the Immortal Nelson died'. One knows exactly who he was – that white faced youth depicted in the famous painting as supporting the mortally wounded Nelson in the cockpit of the Victory. But wait – Purser Burke died in 1815, ten years after Trafalgar, at the age of seventy, so he must have been sixty at the battle; a bit too old for such excitements, I would have said, and not at all a youth at the time. Artist's licence, I presume, and I would not dream of distrusting the inscription. Nor does the village which now proudly proclaims a Burke Drive and a Nelson Close; quite right too and I am sure that none of that long succession of sixty-two rectors of the parish would begrudge Wouldham its recognition of either Purser Burke or Admiral Lord Nelson.

ALDINGTON
St. Martin

Ealda's farmstead

Reached down a muddy lane not far from Romney Marsh, one finds the church surrounded by sheep-dotted fields and pressed against an extensive farmyard – or vice versa. Probably vice versa because the church must antedate the farm; how the latter can have been allowed to crowd the church so intimately on its west and north sides defies my imagination. One supposes that a lord of the manor, possibly even the Archbishop of Canterbury who once had a manor here, may have felt able to appropriate half of the churchyard for his own purposes – at least it was the northern half. Ealda would approve.

The church has Saxo-Norman origins with later additions culminating in post-Victorian battlements at the top of the tower. Externally, it is the 16th century tower that is the most conspicuous feature of the church; it reminded me of the Somerset church towers with their niches for statues and stone-filigreed belfry apertures. Aldington is the only country church in Kent that I can remember having similar tower niches. Here they are empty but what looks very like one of the missing statues now decorates the interior, safe from wind and weather. Inside, one is greeted by evidence of damp and an air of austerity relieved only by elaborately carved pulpit and choir stalls. An absence of memorials confirms the spartan impression but this lack of distinction is more than dispelled by the list of rectors amongst whom I was astonished to find the name 'Erasmus Roterodamus' recorded for the years 1511 and 1512. It seemed incongruous to find a savant of European reputation gracing an out-of-the-world church like Aldington. Erasmus, who does not enjoy an ecstatic press from Bertrand Russell, was forty five and with his best work behind him when rector here. Russell states that he divided his time in England between London (at the home of Sir Thomas More) and Cambridge so I find it difficult to credit Aldington with much of Erasmus' presence in 1511 bearing in mind the problems of country travel in those days. Indeed, in my ignorance, I even suspected that 'Erasmus' was not much more than a 'name-drop' by the church and that the duties of his ministry must have been largely performed by a substitute. Quite by chance, the day after my visit I met someone infinitely better informed than I am and was corrected. Erasmus was frequently in Kent during his stay in England. Moreover, far from being a bucolic desert, Aldington has in the past been a hotbed of literary luminaries. Chesterton, Conrad, Crane and Coward all lived in the neighbourhood at different times but none that I know of are commemorated in the church. Still, the Erasmus association more than makes good the deficiency.

My encounter with Aldington was marred by an all-pervading, soaking mist, interrupted only by sporadic outbursts of even damper rain so my choice of viewpoint was dictated entirely by the necessity of cover. I sat under the lych-gate and the church is represented by no more than the tower. The buildings in the foreground are those of the farmyard and these, together with the handsome churchyard trees, virtually monopolise my paper. I would have preferred, weather and sheep permitting, to attempt a long range view from across the fields from whence the combination of church and farm creates the evocative appearance of a medieval fortress in a solitary landscape. Much more appropriate for a church that can boast Erasmus as rector.

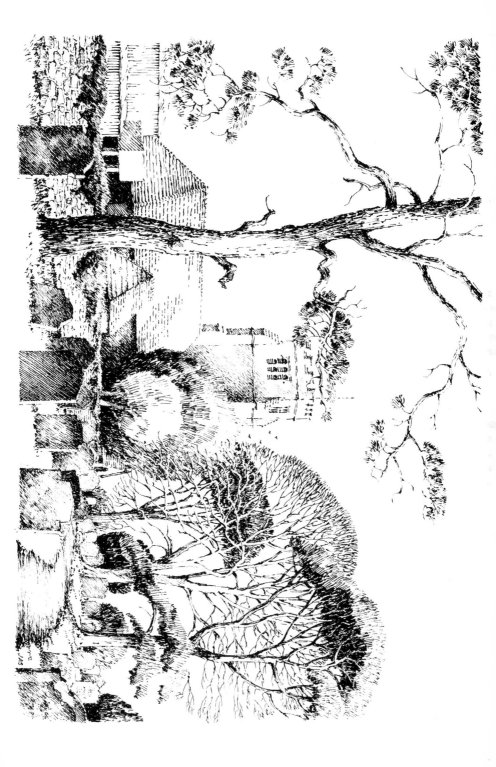

BONNINGTON
St. Rumbold

Buna's farmstead

This little church on the edge of Romney Marsh is so isolated that not one house can be seen from it. Yet it was unlocked when I came to draw it so someone, conscientious to a degree, must come from somewhere twice daily to unlock for the chance visitor and lock again afterwards. I should be surprised if there is much week-day traffic in and out of the church which makes it all the more remarkable and rewarding to find the doors open.

The church is dedicated to St. Rumbold. Rumbold, the Saxon son of a king of Mercia, was born in Northants but lived for no more than three days. During his short span he is credited with crying 'Christianus sum' on D day and preaching a sermon on D plus two. An unlikely achievement, one might suppose, but something unusual must have happened to justify canonization. I wonder what, and why Bonnington church should be devoted to his earthly memory and heavenly protection.

The church and churchyard are tiny; a Norman chancel attached to a small rectangular nave capped at its west end by a lead-covered, ogee-shaped belfry. It is, I believe, the oldest church on Romney Marsh. Apart from its situation and dedication, the features that impressed me were three minute Norman windows, arranged in a triangle at the east end of the chancel, as they are at Barming; the skeletal timber framework for a lofty, but vanished, musicians' gallery under the belfry; and a double-decker pulpit plus sounding board which looked altogether too pompous for Bonnington's rural simplicity. Something more personal endears me to Bonnington, though; a framed notice recording the presence of William van Mildert as assistant curate for the one year 1789/90. I do not think one could have a more inconspicuous or humble ecclesiastical appointment but, nevertheless, van Mildert rose in the hierarchy of the church to achieve the princely See of Durham in 1826 and found Durham University. My interest in him and hence in Bonnington arises from the fact that my daughter belonged to van Mildert College when she was an undergraduate at Durham University. I must persuade her to come and see the little church from which one man rose to great things from so inauspicious a beginning. Van Mildert conveys a message of encouragement for all the aspiring, including my daughter.

I could not resist attempting to include in my sketch of the church the Royal Military Canal which runs below the churchyard and guards the hinterland. I could have wished that the bridge was less functional and more ornamental and in tune with the idyllic and empty Romney Marsh. One might also have preferred the dense cordon of churchyard trees to have obscured rather less of the church but at least the distinctive belfry is visible. Nonetheless as a composition, if not as an identifiable representation, it is satisfying. Not far along the canal stands a World War II pillbox; it is obvious and exposed and only too likely to attract the hostile attention of the enemy. If called upon to repel an invader here, I think I would have chosen to entrust myself to St. Rumbold and the church's Norman walls. It certainly calls for a miracle to expect the Royal Military Canal to hold up the advance of any army.

NEWINGTON
St. Mary

At the risk of offending local susceptibility I would say that this is far too grand a building for its humdrum village on the A2. Fortunately it is sufficiently withdrawn from the road and the 20th century traffic to allow the peace of the countryside to envelop the church undisturbed. It is surprising to find that the church does not keep company with its village astride the road; the latter, once the Roman Watling Street and on the ground before church or village, attracted the parish but not the clergy. I think the clergy has for long had the better of it, to the east and west stretch fruitful orchards and farmland and beyond to the north are the haunting marshes of the Medway estuary. It is only to the south, with its problems of modern ribbon development, that the scene deteriorates visually but it is there, naturally, that the balance of the parish lies and where one would expect the church to be.

It is a good, big, 12th and 13th century church with a long triple roof of nave and north and south aisles. Largely constructed of flint, it is dark and a trifle forbidding in appearance although this impression is softened on the tower by alternating bands of flint and ragstone. Sadly I cannot remark on an interior to which Pevsner devotes respectful attention; my visit was made on a Saturday morning in mid-November when one might, I think, have not unreasonably expected to find an important village church like this open and someone within. Not so; a pale green door (a curious choice of colour) denied entry to anyone so minded.

The churchyard was in very good order I am happy to report. By the gate, without the wall, removed from the church's fabric I believe, stands a sarsen stone, or 'devil stone' as the inscription proclaims. It looks harmless enough but there have been dark deeds hereabouts. Long ago, soon after the Conquest, the nuns of Newington, innocent or guilty alike, suffered the extreme penalty of live burial, at a place macabrely known as Nunpit, for the murder of their prioress.

My visit coincided with a dreadfully damp and dispiriting day. An open air sketch was not a practical possibility, there being no convenient lych-gate for shelter as there had been at Aldington, so the car had to be pressed into use as a mobile studio. For my sketch I retired down the lane to the east, in the direction of Nunpit I dare say, and from the from seat managed the scene you see. The unavoidable foreground, a rather uninspiring smallholding leading up to the churchyard wall, is helpfully mediated by a tangle of blackberry vines and the dead stems of cow parsley. The church itself stands up well against the skyline as, no doubt, its builders intended. The tower is rightly said by Pevsner to be amongst the finest of its type in Kent and I suppose that this place and its church must have once been of more consequence than is the case today, for Thomas à Becket stayed here on his way to Canterbury and defiant martyrdom.

Despite an electoral roll of eighty four, Tudeley cannot be said to be a village church. There is no discernible centre of gravity to the scattered houses and no apparent reason for the church to be where it is. Historically there was iron working in the neighbourhood in the 14th century and the presence then of the necessary medieval population could account for the existence now of this small church in what is today fertile farmland. When I first set eyes on Tudeley church in 1971 the track leading up to it was bordered on one side by a somewhat run-down farmhouse and on the other by decaying barns. Today, thirteen years and much labour later, the farmhouse has been done up and the barns converted into comfortable houses of rural character. This sort of rescue is going on all the time, in southern England at least, and one often wonders what the countryside can have looked like, say in 1920 – a shambles I dare say.

However, to come to the church itself. It is old in origin but little of its beginnings remain beyond some sandstone walling of the nave and chancel. Mostly its exterior must be Georgian including a plain red-brick tower saved by an attractive tiled, octagonal spirelet. The east end of the chancel has suffered most externally, having been reconstructed to accommodate a memorial window. It will need a century or two of weather before it begins to lose its characterless mint condition. Still, I suppose the windows must more than compensate for the modern walling. There are eleven all told in the church, mostly small, and in seven of these, including the memorial, the stained glass is the work of the Russian-born impressionist artist, Marc Chagall.* It is this stained glass, not to everyone's taste, which transforms Tudeley church from an unremarkable parish church without a proper village into a rural museum piece containing major works of art. It is the benefaction of one family who, I imagine, are also responsible for the transformation of the rest of the interior. Here we find all is clean and bright, if a shade clinical – a barrel-vaulted ceiling, painted with a delicate sea-green marbling, and a complete matching set of pews and miniature stalls for the minister which appear Scandinavian in their simplicity and clarity of design. The two ancient memorials which survive are in no way diminished by the admirable modern furnishings or the exotic stained glass.

My sketch of the church makes as much as I can of the railed pair of tombstones in the foreground. I rarely include railings in my pictures, not because they are difficult to draw (which they are) but because they have become something of an endangered species. I do not suppose it was remembered, when sepulchral rails were commandeered for the war effort, how effective they were in discouraging capricious vandalism.

* Now, in 1985, it has been agreed that the remaining four Victorian windows will be replaced by a further four Chagall windows making this church one of only three buildings in the world to have a complete set of stained glass by Marc Chagall.

HARRIETSHAM
St. John the Baptist

Heregeard's water meadow

Harrietsham village confounds convention by lying athwart the main highway. No doubt the road, the A20, is more recent than the bisected village high street so who can have allowed the division? One assumes that this faux-pas occurred before the days of town and country planning and certainly such ruthless treatment would not be countenanced today. At all events those who hurry along the main road with the streaming traffic miss two beautiful survivors of the past — the church to the north and the old village street to the south — and gather a mistaken impression of featureless ribbon development, quite unfair to the real Harrietsham.

From the outside, the church looks larger than it seems when inside. Here the general effect is cosy and I think that the existence of a complete rood screen, with cross above, must be a contributory cause. I was surprised, though, to see a simple table (a communion table?) in the centre on the nave side of the screen. There was no-one in the church, or any explanatory pamphlet, to cast light on this unusual arrangement so I must fall back on my recent reading for a possible explanation. At the time of the Reformation (as I understand it), to give effect to the break with Rome, the authorities in England sought to change the emphasis of the services from mystery and remote ritual towards congregation and comprehension. The altar was relegated to the background and the service concentrated on the preacher in his pulpit and the closely attendant congregation in their box pews. What ceremony there was was conducted about a plain table, not an altar. In time the Victorians reversed this protestanism more or less back towards the Catholic procedure; altars were reinstated and box pews and communion tables swept away. Not here at Harrietsham in the case of the latter and I wondered, in the light of the table in the nave, whether I had stumbled on a rare example of a church clinging to the so-called 'prayer book tradition' of the Reformation. For such to be the case, one would need obstinate and determined clergy and the list of vicars here would seem to support the theory. Almost all churches list their vicars, generally in a discreet, framed notice or on a modest, painted board; Harrietsham, less restrained, favours a forthright listing in the form of an ostentatious wall painting and one cannot help feeling that the incumbents of Harrietsham must have always been very sure of themselves. On the other hand, the position of the mysterious table at the head of the nave may have been some purely temporary arrangement and my suppositions quite wrong. As they say — 'a little learning is a dang'rous thing'.

My sketch was made from the stubble field which separates the church from the northern limit of the village and beyond, a field or two towards the Downs, runs the Pilgrims' Way. The first passer-by that sparkling morning turned out to be the past churchwarden, heavily encumbered by photographic equipment and intent on registering his church on film. Tradition has it, he informed me, that the pilgrims, after gaining spiritual grace in the church, used to restore themselves at a vanished village dispensary before continuing on their way to Canterbury. I did much the same at a nearby pub after the November chill began to bite, but without the justifying excuse of pilgrimage.

In common with many medieval churches, Lenham has been extensively damaged by fire in the distant past. Unlike most, this misfortune was not an act of God but was attributed to malicious damage by 'persons unknown' – an uncertainty that did not prevent an uncompromising sentence of excommunication upon the culprit whoever he may have been. I think it is correct that excommunication permitted, even encouraged, retribution by anyone against the anathematised. A pronouncement therefore against 'persons unknown' would seem to license a general settling of old scores under the pretext that the victim 'was thought to be the culprit'. Anyway, whatever injuries may have been suffered by the innocent of Lenham, their church survived and was repaired. Very well done it was too, for it is now a splendid greystone church in an unspoilt period village. Its immediate surroundings are so attractive that the connoisseurs are inclined to devote as much attention to the heart of this village as they do to the church.

The fire in the church took place in 1299 and so most of the present structure is a 14th century rebuilding. The west tower is solid and secure, but I did notice that the south wall of the nave has a tendency to lean outwards. This vulnerable wall enjoys the prudent support of a regular sequence of buttresses and these will, I hope, take care of gravity and the parallelogram of forces. Lenham church defies convention in that most of the churchyard and the porch lie to the north, but probably it was the monastic establishment, only a fragment of which now remains, which pre-empted the southern, 'devil-free', space around the church. One would have expected the monks to be better equipped to repel Satan than the frailer lay population, but no doubt the former had the greater temporal muscle in the matter of the allocation of church property.

The interior is unusual in possessing a complete regime of box pews and an intricately carved dark mahogany pulpit which, together, echo the Reformation and the 'prayer book' tradition. Nonetheless, the earlier features persist, as they should, being of stone. Actually, according to the church leaflet, they have not so much persisted as been resurrected for the Puritans buried the altar slab below their replacement communion table. Now it takes its rightful place as the chancel altar and keeps company with an equally old, but grander, tombstone altar in the north chapel. One would not presume to adjudicate between the two schools of thought and it is difficult to convey the pleasure and satisfaction that one gains from the contemplation of their symbols.

My drawing scarcely does justice to this church which one would like to portray from more than one angle had one the opportunity. Remembering the south wall and its uncertain tilt, I kept clear and contented myself with a glimpse of the less romantic east end. I was very taken with Lenham churchyard, but one cannot include it all. Here the foreground, largely obscuring the object of my visit, is framed by a yew on one side and by an evergreen on the other. My identification of the evergreen makes it a spruce. There are twenty varieties of spruce in my tree book – tantalisingly difficult to distinguish one from another – but I would like to think that the Lenham specimen is a Brewer's Weeping Spruce, entirely proper to a well stocked churchyard in the hop country.

WORMSHILL
St. Giles

A scattered farming community on top of the Downs with a 12th century church and a 15th century pub — with both of which I am now happily familiar. At first sight the church does not excite one especially being entirely constructed of restored, knapped flints which have not yet had time to recover their lost bloom of antiquity; they will in a century or two. The boarded porch, in contrast, has escaped improvement and sits in comfortable neglect beside the tiny Saxon window in the nave. This porch is remarkable for an entrance formed by the original, but now emaciated, oak timbers naturally shaped into a gothic arch, and also for an unduly elaborate array of rafters and king posts supporting a diminutive tiled roof; equally to scale is the tiny church door which this unassuming porch shelters from the blast.

The church was locked; one could hardly expect otherwise, but the key could be obtained from Court Lodge across the road. I am always diffident about approaching front doors protected by an expanse of lawn and drive — the latter tend to go with pugnacious dogs. To my relief, I found instead the cheerful daughter of the house who came to open the church with a far better grace than I would have managed in similar circumstances. Wormshill church is noted for some rare 14th century stained glass. One is often disconcerted to find how inconspicuous famous things turn out to be in reality and Wormshill's glass is no exception. If I identified it correctly, the celebrated pieces fill the upper lights of the Perpendicular window seen to the left of that large pollarded tree that takes up so much of the foreground of my sketch. More interesting to my mind was the stone pillar font, listed as pre-Norman in the church portable information board, but thoughtfully amplified in pencil by a knowledgeable visitor as a 'Saxon block font'. Two other treasures this church has; the first a bulky 13th century wooden chest for vestments — described as a 'hutch' chest by the display card inside which, incidentally, also warns the reader not to open the lid (fortunately it was open so that one could read the admonition); the second a short length of medieval rood screen propped against the wall. At first I thought what a casual way to treat this relic but, on second thoughts, what else could be done with it? At least it is still there in its proper church to remind us of what there once was. There are not many memorials here, not unusual in a lonely parish like Wormshill, but, of the eight there are, five commemorate rectors which I feel shows a fitting respect for the clergy.

After many excursions to explore the country churches of Kent, I am still unable to understand why they should exert so powerful a fascination. Here at Wormshill one finds a perfectly straightforward and unpretentious structure of a size appropriate to its parish but somehow it stirs my imagination to a far greater extent than, say, a major cathedral like St. Paul's. Why should this be? Perhaps it is something to do with sheer magnitude. One can more easily identify with something less intimidating in scale and more personal in atmosphere. Perhaps it is something to do with continuity. Eight hundred years old, maybe more, Wormshill church, the embodiment of the long religious history of its rural parishioners, is exactly what one has in mind when one thinks of the countryside and the people who have made it what it is.

FRINSTED
St. Dunstan

Fenced in place

An appropriate name for a place in which the church enjoys the protective embrace of a perimeter flint wall — or at least did once. All is in pretty good repair in the south and west quarters of the churchyard but, in the north and east, all that remain of the wall are vestigial brick buttresses. Not that it matters; a drive runs past and, beyond, park-like fields of pasture recede without a blemish into the distance. Punctuating the circumference is a stand of uniformly tall horse chestnut trees; these looked so imposing and bare in the wintry light that I took the time to count them only to discover to my dismay that they number thirteen. I think the missing fourteenth has been supplanted by that sapling, not a chestnut I fear, on the left of the foreground in my sketch. Being unreasonably superstitious, I recommend a fourteenth chestnut as soon as maybe to keep the lightning at bay.

The church was locked but the key could be obtained from the pub facing the church. Imagine my chagrin when I found that this particular inn never opens on Monday mornings. It must be unique. So I had to content myself with a perambulation of the outside and a postponed lunch plus reliance on a previous visit for memory of the interior.

It is a flint church, standard amongst those that line this plateau of the Downs; apparently the nave and chancel were here at the time of William the Conqueror but presumably then built of different materials. It looks in pristine condition today having been thoroughly restored by Sir Gilbert Scott in 1870 with a widening of the north aisle ten years earlier. External evidence of the pre-restoration building can be seen on the south side of the chancel in a blocked priest's doorway exhibiting a characteristically Norman arch. The church is blessed with a prominent square lead sundial half way up the south face of the Perpendicular west tower; mechanical clocks on medieval towers are anachronistic — a sundial is exactly right but too much of a rarity, I am afraid. Frinstead is fortunate to have the one and not the other. Speaking from memory, I seem to remember that the interior, particularly the chancel, has also felt the improving hand of the Victorians and the decorations are certainly striking, not to say extravagant, for a church with an electoral roll of no more than twenty two.

It was in the porch that I read about the size of the electoral register. It was also there that I learnt that the churchwarden finds time to add the duties of Governor of the Bank of England and Lord Lieutenant of the County of Kent to those of his church. I would imagine that the vicar needs to watch his step a bit but at least he can rest easy in so far as the church's finances are concerned; in this respect Frinsted must resemble Kemsing which could also claim a Governor of the Bank amongst its parishioners. Such strength in the management of this church must augur well for its future well-being and one might reasonably hope, I think, that the Almighty could repay the Governor's services to His church in Kent with a little heavenly help from time to time with the finances of the country.

NETTLESTEAD
St. Mary the Virgin

Homestead at a place where nettles grow

The combination of New Year's Day and a brisk north wind would not be everybody's ideal choice for sketching in the open but it gave me a perverse pleasure to defy the elements for an hour or so beside Nettlestead church on the opening day of the year. I have attempted this church more than once, never successfully, but my view on this occasion was dictated by the overriding necessity to have a solid stone wall at my back to temper the worst of the wind.

It is a small church, idyllically sited above the Medway on that brief stretch of the river that is crossed by two medieval bridges and overlooked by four medieval churches. Once this church was the private chapel of Nettlestead Place, the rambling manor house that borders the south side of the churchyard; before that there was a Saxon church here. With the arrival of the de Pympe family, with new ideas stimulated by foreign travel, taking in the battle of Agincourt, the Saxon church was found wanting and was replaced in the early 1400s by the present structure. It is said that the de Pympe of the day, impressed by the stained glass he had seen during his continental campaigns, decided to repeat these architectural felicities in his family chapel at Nettlestead. How did he find time to cultivate a taste for stained glass, fight the battle of Agincourt and return with his life from a very dubious military enterprise? But that is exactly what he did for his short nave here acts as a stone frame for three glorious Perpendicular windows on each side, with the smallish chancel, a later improvement, containing another three, making nine in all. There he and his son installed stained glass to commemorate himself and his friends.

My view is limited to the comparatively primitive west tower which, incidentally, antedates the works of the de Pympes. The wonderful windows, for which the church is so celebrated, are not visible; perfectionists may regret their omission but I find them out of scale and too dominating for this small building which, as commissioned by the de Pympes, is essentially a frame for their stained glass. My attention was attracted to the door at the foot of the tower which has the stamp of extreme antiquity; a gothic-shaped, studded wooden door below a fanlight of decorated stone tracery, the whole crumbling and of diminutive proportions more suited to the physique of the Normans than to our own. My pleasure in this elaborate little doorway was unexpectedly reduced on learning that it was rescued from the demolition of the old church at Teston by the then vicar who held both livings in plurality.

The church was locked but in the fortress-like south porch, another de Pympe commission, there was pinned a notice from the Bishop of Rochester, dated March 1984, sequestrating the tithes, rents, emoluments etc. attaching to the church lest they be 'wasted or embezzled' there being no incumbent — a pronouncement to which the churchwardens might justifiably take exception, I would have thought. It is sad to think that the Church and Nettlestead are so reduced; Reginald de Pympe and his son, John, the creators of this abandoned jewel beside their manor house must wonder, if they can, why they ever bothered but with luck they may be enjoying their reward elsewhere. At the very least they are assured of a sort of immortality in stone.

Stream known as 'Hlyde' – the noisy one

Whenever the names Leeds and Kent are linked it is the fairy-tale moated castle that comes to mind, and rarely is the church on the hill above ever considered. And yet the church is almost as striking in its way and with the inestimable boon that it is spared the blight of tourists and fund-raising activities.

Approaching the church one is confronted by a massive square tower, one of the most substantial in Kent. This construction is early Norman with walls six to eight feet thick. Not content with the elephantine walls, later pessimists added buttresses to match – why they should be necessary is beyond me. The quoins of this tower, says the guide, are made of 'tufa', a stone that cuts like cheese when first quarried but conveniently hardens on exposure to the air. This it certainly must have done, for the tower has been standing for 800 years or so with no sign of strain, unless of course, those buttresses are concealing something. The tower is crowned by a restrained little spirelet, which, with its four dormer windows at the cardinal points, provides a later refinement to the robust simplicity of the Norman architecture. To complete the inventory of the remarkable features of this tower one must go inside to see how the Normans joined it to the Saxon nave that preceded it. It was done with a columned arch of majestic, cathedral proportions. There was then a priory here at Leeds and its presence may account for the generous dimensions that give this village church such dignity. The castle in the valley may have had something to do with it too.

It is hardly fair to reward a church that is open to the chance visitor like myself with words of criticism but there are two 'improvements' here that diminish the original interior. The first is the floor of the nave and aisles. This consists of handsome grey flagstones interspersed with inscribed ledger stones; fine but where the pews would normally stand the beautiful stone floor has been covered by a dull wooden platform on which chairs now rest. The second criticism concerns the south chapel which dates from the 14th century. Here a medieval chamber is virtually obliterated by a Victorian organ. I believe that, at the time of its installation, the village musicians objected – perhaps there would be objections now if the organ were to be removed from the chapel to be replaced by music on records as backing for the hymns. Not all innovation is misguided and one that involved the return of the chapel to its proper function would seem to me to be entirely beneficial.

Enough of these carping complaints about an ancient landmark. To compensate for the offending organ, the church is one of the few to retain a complete rood screen separating the chancel and chapels from the nave and aisles. This is an elegant carved wooden barrier simulating arched windows below a vaulted ceiling and having the effect of a curtain between congregation and clergy. As such it would seem to contradict the aims of the church; is it not presumptuous, though, to question the purposes of any organisation capable of creating and sustaining all these wonderful buildings?

MONKS HORTON   *Filthy or muddy farmstead*
St. Peter

True to its name there is a farmstead, Horton Court, immediately across the lane from this little church but I hardly think that either deserves the description given by the Anglo-Saxons. The farm had, like all farms in January, mud about but nothing to complain of and the church in its neat, walled churchyard can surely be described as trim. All around are fields rising to the Downs above. It is pure unalloyed countryside with all the advantages thus implied or, as some might say, but not me, the disadvantages. Presumably it is the 'Horton' that carries the muddy aspersion; the 'Monk's' derives from the nearby priory, I take it. This was a Cluniac foundation, established in the reign of Henry II and disestablished in the reign of Henry VIII by which time there remained only six on the strength. But even so few must have practised, I am sure, a sufficiently efficient standard of farm management to make the Saxon name a disparaging misnomer. The monks did have their own church or chapel in the priory, and considering the emptiness of the country round about, I am surprised that there was a need for two places of worship virtually within bow-shot of each other.

St. Peter's is not elaborate. It is Early English, says Pevsner, and consists of a simple nave and chancel in flint and stone enclosed in an evergreen churchyard. My view is somewhat obstructed by the yews but that riven trunk on the left, over-shadowing the path, conveys exactly the atmosphere of antiquity and longevity that all good churchyards should have. The church was locked but, although the key was available from Horton Court, I somehow did not fancy an encounter with farmyard dogs on their home ground. Pevsner speaks of no more than the chancel arch and a helm inside so I do not think I was too deprived. The external features that attracted my attention were all on the unshown, north side – a tiny, blocked doorway, the projecting treads of a vanished rood staircase and a chimney stack to what I presume is the vestry. The church was restored in the 1840s (why?) and the walls have, I am afraid, exchanged the romantic patina of centuries for the clinical look of yesterday, no doubt in the praiseworthy interests of weather proofing. Pevsner says that the plain Victorian bell-gable (almost invisible in my sketch) replaced a wooden structure like that at High Halden. I cannot decide whether the replacement is an improvement or not – neither arrangement is particularly distinguished in my opinion but I suppose that the High Halden tower is the more unusual and noteworthy. It is highly rated by experts like the late Alec Clifton-Taylor.

There is no porch, entry being made between the two buttresses that prop the west end. Here there was a notice announcing the forthcoming Visitation of the Bishop of Maidstone to discuss the future of this church. The bishop's descent was not dated by year but I imagine that it preceded my visitation in January 1985 and that a decision has by now been reached. It would seem to the uncommitted observer like myself that redundancy awaits St. Peter's and that it will follow the priory into religious oblivion. I am glad to have seen it while all is still intact and in working order, so to speak.

St. Mary

Not an easy church to find, for St. Mary's is separated from its village by the 'minnis', an expanse of common woodland which I was told I would be unable to cross by car but must go round. Described as 'bleak and lonely' by Glynne, the Victorian authority, I did not find it so at all. There are pleasant fields around and five flint and stone cottages stand compactly beside the churchyard gate. I imagine that they were once estate cottages for they are all of a character and solidly built.

The church itself is also compact and seems to hug the ground. The fabric is Early English, flint reinforced by brick at all the danger points with quoins or buttresses. The tower, which looks impregnably strong, if abbreviated, has the curious feature of a tile-hung south face. Normally there is not much behind hanging tiles, a timber frame, laths and plaster perhaps, which is what we have in part of my house but not what you would expect in a tower built in the 13th century. What happened to the stone or flint? Possibly the tiles hide a wartime accident – not impossible here below the flight path across Kent from the coast; Pevsner makes no comment and most of the other reference authorities whom I consulted ignore this church entirely.

In common with many experts, they are not infallible. Notwithstanding the sturdy, confident exterior, I found the interior even more deserving of notice. Here is a surprise – although, observing its 'bleak and lonely' situation, maybe not so surprising – a complete layout of box pews in both nave and aisle. Painted a calm, refreshing grey and white, this unreconstructed arrangement for the congregation is dominated by a three-decker mahogany pulpit. Clearly sermons were the order of the day at Stelling Minnis and I would classify this church as a 'prayer book' church which the reformers must have overlooked. There is also a gallery facing the pulpit, not the altar, which I take to be confirmation of my amateur analysis. I could find only two memorials inside the church, one a worn and indecipherable stone tablet, the other to a past churchwarden. The local gentry must be commemorated elsewhere and very likely their disregard of St. Mary's accounts for the preservation of the box pews. Vicars likewise appear to have been uninterested – there is no list of them that I could discover in my brief inspection (charitably, my wife suggested that the list might have gone to be cleaned). Other noteworthy simplicities here are a floor of uniform, brick-red tiles, an elegant font and spindly king posts supporting a barrel ceiling. To sum up, the interior of this church has an unspoilt, unsophisticated charm that I found very beguiling and the opposite of bleak and lonely.

Stelling Minnis is only some eight miles south of Canterbury down the Roman road. The countryside round about is sparsely populated and I doubt if the church or village have ever commanded much attention in the deaneries and chapters. That might explain the unreconstructed interior but it fails to explain the extensive reinforcing brickwork outside or the tile-hung tower. It is a nice little puzzle and doubt-less my speculations are well wide of the mark. One is intrigued here by a remote church that seems to be out of step with the general run of its contemporaries throughout Kent.

'Capel cum Tudeley with Five Oak Green', to give it its full description in the latter half of the 20th century, is little more than a chapel which, apparently, it originally was. Tudeley, comprising a pub and a scattering of farm cottages just over a mile to the west, and the senior member of the triumvirate, is itself not much more than a miniature as can be seen from the drawing facing page 50. As one looks at the countryside hereabouts it is not immediately obvious why little Tudeley should have needed to bolster its situation with a subordinate chapel but that is what is reputed to have happened in the distant past and now the two are linked by geography, by the one incumbent and, I think, if memory serves, by the same electoral roll of eighty four. Tudeley is mentioned in the Domesday Book, Capel not, but from the existence of a Norman window Mr. Newman dates the latter as originating at least before 1200. The Normans had given way to the Angevins by then but I daresay that the distinctive style of architecture attributed to the Norman reign lingered on, particularly in rural areas like the Medway valley east of Tonbridge.

As with so many churches, Capel has experienced a history of destruction and rebuilding. Lightning in 1639 destroyed most of the church with the result that the uncompromising, four-square tower was rebuilt in the 17th century and the south wall of the nave in the 19th. Oddly enough these two reconstructions are today the most attractive parts of the church but the rest is a sorry disappointment. The tower looks exactly right to me; seen from the west (not my view) there is, just above the west door, a dear little double-lancet ogee window which dates from the original, pre-fire, lower half of the tower. I wish I could have transferred this window to the south face. The 19th century nave wall of honey-coloured sandstone blocks harmonises agreeably with the grey tower, its red-tiled pyramid roof and the enclosing dark green yews. Its windows are still a trifle too pristine but time and weather will remedy that. The rest of the exterior, though, is a sad story. The chancel, said to be of Norman origin, and the north wall of the nave, where the Norman window is to be found, have both been hidden by a comprehensive coat of cement rendering that looks only too like some modern economy construction. Fortunately the north side of the church is more or less inaccessible and the chancel heavily screened by evergreens; although its blemishes are thus mercifully obscured, poor little Capel has suffered treatment that can only be described as cruel. Anything, almost, would be better.

Without being in any way an authority on the subject, I suppose it was the threat of damp which justified the cement for on the other side of the rendered walls there is a vulnerable stretch of medieval narrative wall paintings that lifts Capel to the same artistic plane as its senior partner, Tudeley of the Chagall windows. One might say that, here, the outside may have been sacrificed for what lies inside and many would say that this is reason enough at Capel. As it is locked on a week-day, one is deprived of the paintings and presented instead with a warm, charming-looking little countryside church.

BRENZETT
St. Eanswith

Brenzett on Romney Marsh presents an appropriately worn and weathered face to the world; when I sketched the church in February the world consisted of myself and a few sheep grazing in the adjacent fields. Not a soul moved, not a dog barked and no birds flew that I can remember. Nevertheless the slumbering church made a picture; old grey rubblestone walls relieved by herringbone masonry from the days of the Normans and topped by roofs of warm red tiles with a blackened broach spire acting as a western finial. The porch is the most rubbly of all and, although eminently solid and serviceable, it is one of the most rough and ready stone entrances that I can recall. The earliest part of the church, 12th century, is the south wall which faced me from where I drew and the most recent, 20th century, is that angled buttress at the south east corner of the chancel. The porch and spire date from the 15th century, with the latter being restored to the perpendicular in 1902 when much interior restoration was undertaken. This church continues to receive attention, witness a somewhat dog-eared notice in the porch which records that the church was 'redecorated as a gift by the Office Cleaning Services Ltd. of London EC1'. One wonders what their connection with Brenzett can have been.

Wonderful to relate the church was open and provided a scholarly guide. Compared to the mellow exterior, the interior is not particularly exciting – perhaps the restoration of 1902 has something to answer for here. However, no-one could fail to notice the grandiose alabaster memorial to a recumbent father and son and nor should one miss the Norman chevron moulding that runs up the jamb of the chancel arch.

The dedication to St. Eanswith, a very minor saint, aroused my interest. Happily the pamphlet is enlightening. Apparently Eanswith was the grand-daughter of King Ethelbert; after completing her novitiate as a nun, she set about founding the first nunnery in England in 630 AD. It was during the building of this establishment that she performed her first miracle by extending a timber beam using the power of prayer alone. She later restored sight to a blind woman and capped that by causing water to run uphill from Cheriton to Folkestone. Ten years later, at the relatively youthful age of twenty six, she was dead if the attribution of bones unearthed in a Folkestone church is correct. We know that life expectation must have been very limited in Eanswith's day and consequently that life was lived at an intense pace in the few years available but the saint does seem to have accomplished a great deal in her eight years of adult life. Reluctant as I am to accept these legends as fact, one must concede that the young royal abbess must have been active to an uncommon degree to achieve canonisation, even for someone of her high rank. Her history puts one in mind of St. Rumbold of Bonnington church, a few miles away, who is also credited with miraculous feats in a very brief life. Neither saint operated in the immediate vicinity of the church dedicated to their memory – is it something peculiar to Romney Marsh churches that persuades them to adopt unsung and obscure saints?

APPLEDORE
St. Peter and St. Paul

At the apple tree –
or a piece of land reclaimed from the sea. Which?

My view of this church is not, I think, the best available. Cold was my enemy; I just could not forsake the comfort of the car for the freezing February air. Here one sees the church on its eminence above the Royal Military Canal and this is the memory of Appledore church that will probably be carried away by all who enter Romney Marsh by the road from Tenterden. A more conventional close-up is obtained from the wide village street from which one is confronted by the uncompromising 13th century west tower. I regret its omission from my collection; it is unusual in possessing vacant statue niches and two eccentric quatrefoil windows beside the off-centre belfry aperture. The church was open but an inner door politely asked to be kept closed 'to keep out the birds'. Lucky Appledore if birds are all there is to worry about now – not so once as this church is the successor to a victim of the French in 1380.

Inside there is an air of spaciousness and a corresponding chill. The floor, always an important feature, looked more attractive than many and for this we have to thank the restoration in the 1920s when the Victorian tiles were removed (hurrah) to reveal their more presentable predecessors. The Victorian pews were also removed at this time to be replaced by the present oak pews. There are not too many of the latter, understandably, and possibly their scarcity contributes to the air of space. It has also encouraged the parishioners (or the WI) to provide a comprehensive set of embroidered hassocks. However the eye-catching feature retained here is a medieval rood screen covering both nave and aisles to which have been added seven painted armorial shields. These represent two kings – Richard II, in whose reign the present church was built, and King George V; two archbishops of Canterbury – Stephen Langton and Randall Davidson (but not Warham whose arms are displayed above the door he caused to be made in the west tower); the two saints – St. Peter, crossed keys, and St. Paul, crossed swords; and St. Martin's Priory, Dover, which was the patron here until Cranmer took the church under Canterbury's wing at the time of the Reformation.

Appledore and its church may look peaceful enough today, although I suspect that the summer tourists often disturb the calm. It has not always been so. First the Danes invaded, coming inland up the River Rother (before its channel became diverted to Rye) to build a fort in 892 AD; the French followed in 1380 to burn and destroy – hence the replacement Early English church which stands today; and Jack Cade's army (mob?) passed through the village in 1450. Since those turbulent days, peace, but with sufficient cause for alarm to prompt the building of the defensive canal in 1804 and concrete pillboxes in 1940. There must always have existed something of a front line feeling here on the edge of the Marsh.

One wonders if the French teach their children about the attack on Appledore in the same spirit that we are taught to remember Harfleur by those inspiring words that Shakespeare put into the mouth of Henry V during his assault. Perhaps not, as both expeditions appear, by hindsight to have been pointless and spiteful and are only transformed as glorious if there is a poet to immortalise them. Appledore is testimony to the French raid and the recovery therefrom.

The hamlet of Burmarsh, on Romney Marsh, was originally a Saxon settlement and on one occasion, it is said, the manor was sold by a grandson of King Ethelwulf to a friend for 4000 pence; translated into pounds, £40, this transaction reminds us of the staggering extent to which the nominal value of the currency has changed over the years. This church too; the early parts are Norman but the generously buttressed tower in Perpendicular and what is now the chancel is thought to have once been a Saxon chapel. Externally, one is surprised to find that an unpretentious village like Burmarsh should possess a church with battlements lining the parapet of the nave. I wonder if the French raid on Appledore could have inspired the pseudo-fortifications. These battlements produce an odd effect by hiding the ridge of the nave roof without obscuring the top of the chancel roof; one has the impression of a hollow-backed church, something that is not apparent from the inside. However the feature that makes a visit to Burmarsh obligatory for ecclesiologists is the church doorway within the simple porch. This is pure Norman, I think, exhibiting the semi-circular arch, embroidered by the characteristic zigzag moulding, and decorated, if that is the right word, by a grinning, grimacing head as the keystone. It is not a doorway that anyone could overlook and I was unable to judge whether the keystone head was intended to be welcoming or minatory; it must once have warned the sinful to repent. I made sure that the old wooden door did not involuntarily slam fast behind me when I entered.

Within, there is not much to see. In extent, the church, which consists of no more than a slim nave and chancel, is distinctly compact and belies the general impression given by the outside of a more substantial building. Still, the village is no more than a hamlet and I am sure that all who wish to attend can readily be accommodated. Of memorials there are few and none to anyone of historic consequence. I was, though, diverted to see a small framed notice bearing the Admiralty's foul anchor above the words:

'Presented by the Lords of Commissioners of
the Admiralty to the Civil Parish of Burmarsh
to commemorate the adoption of HMS Romney
during Warship Week, 1942.'

When I returned home I looked up the Romney. She was a Bangor class minesweeper of 672 tons, built in 1940 and scrapped in 1950. I have no doubt she rendered valuable service, giving the parishioners of Burmarsh every reason to be proud of their adopted warship.

In contrast to the bare walls of the nave, the hospitable inn adjoining the church-yard, the Shepherd and Crook, where my wife, dog and I had lunch, displayed a tattered shirt of chain mail and armoured gauntlets of the same period. These accoutrements gave the pub an air of the medieval world to match that of the ancient church and seemed to confirm the existing bond of proximity and isolation. I was not therefore entirely surprised to read in the church pamphlet that, while the church was being restored in 1876, services were held in the Shepherd and Crook. Excellent. I wonder if this temporary arrangement increased the size of the congregation and, if so, whether the increase was permanent.

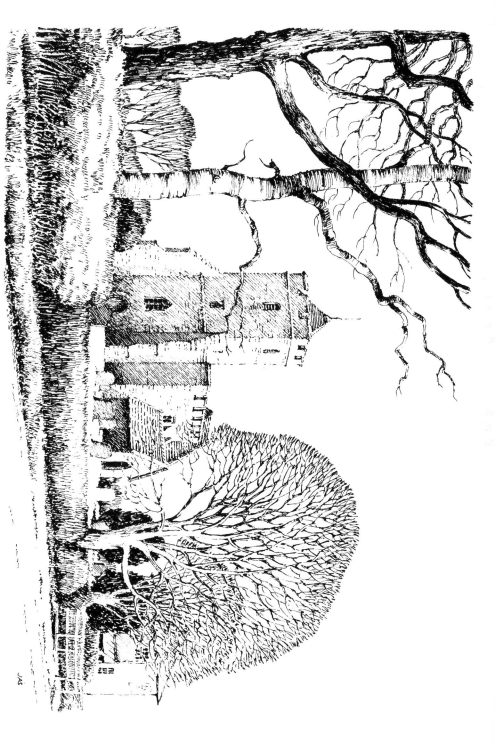

The impression given by this church as one approaches up the open churchyard is one of lean height. It could be the tall spire and the absence of aisles together with the steep pitch of nave and chancel roofs which create the somewhat sinewy, towering appearance. Despite a suggestion of Victorian church architecture, it is an old church of rubblestone walls displaying remnants of herring-bone courses near ground level. The tower is 13th century, though maybe the spire is an afterthought, and there are Norman windows; as a building, it improves the closer the inspection.

However, I found that it is the interior here which is to be preferred. The nave and chancel are high and narrow reflecting the exterior silhouette and there are no unnecessary frills to mar the medieval austerity. Four things stand out in my memory: first, two pairs of corbel stumps which Pevsner surmises are all that remains of the rood screen in the nave and the 'Lenten veil' in the chancel (the latter, I believe, was a curtain hung in front of the altar, presumably in Lent); second, traces of wall paintings framed under glass for protection − a pity as the glass effectively diminishes the air of antiquity; third, a handsome matching set of carved, buttressed pews; and most important, a unique square dedication stone of enormous but uncertain age. This little tablet, inscribed with six lines of cryptic but decipherable Latin lettering, speaks, to me at least, with the authentic voice of the early years of Christianity in this country.

In the porch we are brought back to 1985 with a bang. Here is exhibited a sort of tariff of charges that reminds one of those itemised menus, written in an unmistakable gallic hand, that one sees outside restaurants. I noted these service charges for the benefit of an antiquarian who might chance to read these lines, say, in the next century. For instance, today (1985) the reading of banns costs £4, the marriage service £33, baptism £2, the funeral service £18 with burials in the churchyard ranging between £18 and £24.

Postling church is not set in the world of mammon; never has been if Glynne's disparaging comment in 1877 of 'a wretched and poverty-stricken place' is to be believed. It does not give that impression today. Immediately bordering the churchyard on the south are the magnificent barns of Postling Court (under repair when I was there) and to the north rise the timeless Downs. Folkestone is not far away but the hamlet of Postling seems like a precious oasis in which progress has been ignored and, unless the prospective channel tunnel does something awful, there is no reason why there should be any change to its idyll.

PADDLESWORTH
St. Oswald

Paeddel's enclosure

Of the two Paddlesworths in Kent, the church dedicated to St. Oswald on the crown of the Downs above Folkestone is incomparably the finer. Both churches are Saxo-Norman but the Snodland version, having done duty as a farm barn in its time, is barely recognisable as a church. This hilltop ancient has clearly always been one and may still be in use as such although I would not like to bet on that.

Both Paddlesworths are downland churches. Here in East Kent there is a crossroads, a pub, and about a dozen houses and cottages to make up the hamlet. The church itself is set back and screened by a majestic pair of oaks. One approaches by a narrow path between fields conscious of the shadowed chapel beyond the looming trees. At least, one is in winter; in summer when the leaves are out, I imagine the church is completely hidden. In winter there is an intriguing air of beckoning mystery as one makes one's way up the path, in summer the church must spring as an enchanting surprise from behind its green curtain. In either season one cannot fail to be captivated by the setting of this isolated, thousand-year-old church.

Not unnaturally, it is very small and simple, consisting of a nave, thirty five feet long, and a chancel eleven feet long. Its height is in proportion but nevertheless the west end, with its diminutive bellcote, demands three buttresses for stability. There are Norman windows placed somewhat haphazardly, no porch but north and south Norman doorways. The north door is relatively plain — visible here in the sketch — but the south door is more ambitious with decorated, contrasting shafts to support the horizontal lintel. Both openings are tiny and looked as if they had not been used for some time. As I prowled around the outside I was rewarded by spotting a scratch dial on one of the quoin stones. I am not clear how it would have worked but these 14th or 15th century radial scratches were apparently used to announce the time of the next service.

Being so small, the windows were accessible and one could see inside. From what I could make out, the unplastered walls revealed the same rough rubblestone and flint texture as the more weathered outside. I could see no memorials but the spartan interior was relieved by rows of wooden pews, each with its poppy-head bench end and tally plate to show who presented it. One could sense a relatively massive Norman chancel arch restricting vision from the nave and necessitating the provision of a squint, something which would hardly seem necessary for a church with a maximum breadth of sixteen feet.

When my wife and I found this beguiling church we had only one disappointment. After a satisfactory lunch in the pub, we emerged with our sketching paraphernalia to find that a freezing sea mist had developed. I could just manage a quick rough but my wife's watercolours were waterlogged. And all the while we could hear the boom of the Folkestone foghorn. It sounded incongruous, three miles inland, and, in fact, the only times I have ever heard a foghorn have been when ashore, never at sea. Like Paddlesworth church, foghorns are things of the past and both in their way stimulate one's romantic imaginings.

Surrounded by orchards on its hilltop, the only word to describe this place is gorgeous. Here one sees a rectangle of green grass framed on the south side by the church, dark against the sky; on the east by the manor, on the north by the wealden pub and on the west, by farmyard oasts. What could be better, particularly since the manor and the churchyard merge with no defined boundary. I had difficulty in deciding which view to draw as the church looked equally attractive from any angle. In the end, I settled in the churchyard/manor with my chair hard against the manor's battlemented south front. It was not obvious whether or not I was thus trespassing on the manor's domain but I was definitely among the tombstones.

When I had finished my rough sketch, an elderly man emerged from the recesses of the churchyard and introduced himself as a churchwarden with the offer of a conducted tour of the church. Needless to say I was delighted. St. Michael's is a consistently Perpendicular church grafted onto an earlier chapel, the latter dedicated to St. Stephen and founded in 1120. One wonders why the dedication was changed but it is almost all St. Michael now and very little of St. Stephen remains. The enlargement was an act of gratitude on the part of the lady of the manor for the safe return of her husband, John Martyn, and her son from the battle of Agincourt. How lucky we are that they should have survived to be so splendidly and permanently commemorated.

Their enduring memorial is a flint church comprising chancel and north and south chapels divided from nave and aisles by a complete rood screen. Centuries later Lady Martyn's benefactions were emulated, albeit on a reduced scale, by successors at the manor when the chancel and north chapel were extended in the 19th and 20th centuries. These extensions are subtle and unobtrusive, the Perpendicular windows being retained and simply shifted horizontally to the east.

My churchwarden guide was punctilious in pointing out matters of interest; there were the elegant, shafted pillars flanking the nave, not of Bethersden marble as is generally reported; the 17th century pewter flagon, paten and alms dish, now carefully preserved in the 12th century aumbry, but which were found up in the rafters when the roof was being repaired; the iron-bound churchwardens' chest which looked as if it might have been used as an ammunition box at Agincourt but apparently dates from 1691 — virtually yesterday in terms of Hernhill; the portrait of Parson Handley who called out the constabulary in 1838 to arrest, and incidentally kill, mad Tom 'Courtney', an unbalanced local nuisance; and something I should certainly have missed — a stonemason's signature, a delicately carved oak leaf on the jamb of a doorway.

The churchwarden was eager to inform and justifiably proud of his charge. One never ceases to be astonished by those untutored 'primitives' of the 15th century, who without benefit of modern technology, still managed to produce buildings of far greater beauty and permanence than anything we can achieve today. This medieval church is an exemplar and I cannot feel that either my sketch or commentary do justice to its merits.

St. Cosmas and St. Damian

Coming direct from the graces of Hernhill, as I did, Blean church was an anti-climax. Possibly this is not being fair to Blean which was built on a far less generous scale than Hernhill. Surrounded by fields, well apart from its village and abandoned by its parishioners in flight from the Black Death (my deduction, as very little scholarship is devoted to Blean by the authorities I consult in the public library), Blean can never have enjoyed the support of patrons sufficiently rich or pious to endow and embellish their church in the centuries when this was the thing to do. So what we have here is an unambitious 13th century flint building of modest nave and chancel with, surprisingly, a north aisle added in 1866 to match the nave. What can conceivably have prompted that addition, I wonder – a 19th century population explosion or a latter day patron?

In plan and outline, apart from the Victorian aisle, Blean is very similar to little Paddlesworth. Whoever looks after it now, though, cannot have much sympathy for the past. The door to the uninspiring porch was locked and painted pale green (a double fault!) and the cement rendering surrounding the adjacent 14th century nave windows, light grey – an unfortunate combination of colours. A black door and the removal of the cement to reveal the flint beneath would do much to restore the character of this medieval building, I think. On the north side, even more misguided, a modern wooden church hut has been installed in close proximity. With plenty of room in the churchyard and an adequate growth of evergreen trees, this modern anachronism could easily have been accommodated out of sight.

Just as at Paddlesworth, I could make out some of the interior through the lancet windows of the chancel. Inside it looked every bit as severe as the outside. From what I could see, the altar consisted of a table covered by a green baize cloth enclosed within bare, white-washed walls. There was a feeling of puritan iconoclasm here but I may be doing the church an injustice for I could not see much of the nave where things may be better.

The curious fact is that, although Blean church and its surroundings looked deprived in comparison with Hernhill, I find that my sketch of Cinderella Blean makes it look just as attractive and that, in a way, may contradict everything said above. I have taken care, of course, to omit the anathematised, but useful, church hut and, fortunately from where I sat in a field to the west, I was unable to see the bleak outlines of what I look to be the university buildings of Canterbury to the east so it could be said that an element of artist's licence has been called in aid of this medieval survivor from the days before the Plague. If I have been over-critical of Blean, I must plead the locked porch door and an aversion to the close imposition of the 20th century on the defenceless 13th and this may have influenced my judgement. If so, apologies to Blean.

With Watling Street, now less imaginatively named the A2, only some hundreds of yards away, one would naturally expect Bapchild's church to convey an air of antiquity and longevity. And so it does, notwithstanding the distant roar of passing traffic. Local history claims a timber Saxon predecessor here and a council of king and chapter in 694 AD — no doubt to settle such material matters as the division of taxes and tithes. The present church dates from the Normans.

Almost entirely made of rough flint walls, reinforced by regular stone quoins, it presents a mellow, cared-for appearance. I was particularly gratified, after I had circled the outside and mentally assigned Tudor brickwork to the little porch, to read in the church history that this entrance was added in 1523. My self-esteem was further flattered to have my perception of the shadows of Norman windows around the recent east window of the chancel confirmed by the all-seeing Pevsner. The only criticism I could possibly make of the external appearance of this church concerns the broach spire which looks overbearing and was, I suspect, an afterthought. (Perhaps it was the presence of Rodmersham church in the next parish that provoked Bapchild with the competitive addition.) Despite this minor cavil, St. Lawrence's church, behind its picket fence and hollowed, pollarded chestnuts, looks exactly as one would like a village church to look — old, weather-beaten and enduring.

Inside, if anything, it is more interesting than outside. The position of the tower and the suggestion of a gothic arch behind that brickwork at its base has led experts to conclude that the blocked arch once gave on to an apsidal chancel in which services were held, perhaps before the Norman construction. For quite a small church Bapchild provides an abundance of portly pillars to separate nave and aisle — eight in all, five of which are Norman and octagonal, three Early English and round. To me, this mini-forest of piers spoke clearly of those unscientific days when builders relied on mass to achieve stability rather than on mathematical theory. The arcade may obstruct the view of the chancel and that could explain the recent relegation of the rood screen from its proper position to the wall of the north chapel. Still visible on the walls and piers, lit by the coloured rays of light filtering through the stained glass, one can make out the faded traces of wall painting — the charm of which I consider sufficient excuse to quote R.L. Stevenson's phrase of 'painted windows and storied walls' in this account of my visit.

Last and most curious, a mammoth's tooth is displayed in a small glass case below an empty statue niche on one of the pillars. The tooth was found when they built the church but, as my wife pertinently observed, what of the rest of the creature? Anyway, this relic of prehistory is preserved in a suitably antique setting but it seems wayward of a church to accommodate the animal while denying the saint his sanctuary.

Less than one mile to the south of Bapchild, Rodmersham church cannot possibly summon much of a congregation today and I doubt if it ever has. The village houses which line the road beside the church are few, even if for the most part handsome and generous, but there is no pub or village shop. There was an air of anonymity and reserve about Rodmersham on the day I was there; no-one moved and I felt alone and solitary in the shadow of this church.

The church porch was welcoming; at least the painted garlands above the inner door, proclaiming that 'This is none other than the House of God', were. Sadly the welcome stopped there for the old door was firmly locked. Reference to the never-failing Pevsner tells me that I was denied a view of the rare 15th century wooden canopied sedilia, a Victorian rood screen and a coffin slab against a wall. It would appear, though, that the exterior is more rewarding than the interior for a familiar of Kent's medieval churches, of whom I must now count myself as one. So back to the long grass of the churchyard. The overriding impression given by the church is that of dark, knapped-flint walls, in good order on the south and east fronts, pleasantly worn and irregular to the west and north. The tower dominates the silhouette, and indeed the countryside as well, and according to Arthur Mee is 'one of the best 15th century towers in Kent'. Not only do its diagonal supporting buttresses run to four stages but, from the string course below the battlements, there leans a complete complement of menacing gargoyles. The tower has a south east stair turret but no weather vane that I could see – a pity – but also no clock to mar its purity – a good thing in my opinion. The north side of the church, the subject of my sketch, is remarkable for a small external turret to the roof loft and a little blocked doorway guarded by a dwarfish, grinning stone head. I did not particularly take to the dwarf but the rood-loft turret seemed to me the best thing about this church after the dominant Perpendicular west tower.

Considering the present size of the village, the church is more than adequate and, at its foundation, must have represented a financial Everest in terms of building costs; I suspect an outside subvention, possibly from Canterbury. One would imagine that the population has always been scattered and, with several other churches of the period almost within bell ringing range, one wonders what induced the very considerable outlay needed. As a conspicuous feature of the countryside, the church is justification enough today; what other priorities took second place to building expenditure we can never know.

Still surrounded by the sheep-grazed orchards which aroused the favourable comments of Glynne in 1877, Rodmersham cannot have changed much in the last hundred years – or even the last six hundred.

MILSTEAD
St. Mary and the Holy Cross

Milk place

Milstead church stands on what seems like a tree-lined islet at the centre of its minuscule hamlet with the road running round below and acting as a sort of moat. It is a fact that one often sees a village church embanked in its churchyard above the surrounding roads, never below; the church obviously preceded the road and primacy of establishment seems to have been repeated in contour levels where possible. It is almost as if the original designers had had the 20th century and its ceaseless traffic in mind when they laid out the church and churchyard. Although hardly Piccadilly, Milstead is one of many beneficiaries of this far-sighted arrangement.

This is, I believe, a basically Early English church, Pevsner says the nave and tower are Perpendicular, the rest earlier but much restored. I would hesitate to disagree but the tower looked pre-Perpendicular for three reasons; one, there are no buttresses, two, the stonework is rough and ready and three, the quoins are laid on the 'long and short' principle (for us non-experts, 'long and short quoins' are laid alternately flat and on end), a practice which I understand signifies Saxon work. I expect I have got it wrong but it would be nice to think not.

I do not know about the porch. It looks a neat little place but did not seem to me to be properly bonded to the church itself — just the sort of botched job I might do if I attached a porch to a building and not what one generally sees from medieval masons. The inner door was locked (and the keeper of the key being out, there was no entry for me); I would have liked to have opened this old door — it is double-hinged, something I have not seen before.

As with Rodmersham, explored before lunch, it was back to the churchyard which here is spacious and equipped with a sort of summer house. At the time of my visit it was carpeted with daffodils, snowdrops, crocuses and primroses — all in flower. It seemed entirely appropriate that all these spring flowers should grace a rural churchyard and I was fortunate to find them in bloom.

In the midst of all this vegetation, I stumbled on a large horizontal slab inscribed as the entrance to the Tylden family vault. The Tyldens lived in the Tudor manor house opposite and one of the sons was killed at the battle of Alma in the Crimea. After two years his body was brought back here to be interred in the family vault, says Arthur Mee. Visualising the chaotic carnage of a Russian battlefield and its aftermath, one hopes it was the body of young Tylden and not that of some Cossack Tartar who also perished on that day. Milstead war memorial provides a second example of uncertain identity. Here are recorded, above the claim that 'their name liveth for evermore', the names of the ten servicemen who fell in the 14/18 and 39/40 wars. Unhappily the letters of one name have been dislodged so there is one identity that has already been lost. Churchyards, with their indecipherable tombstones, are everywhere elegiac repositories of the departed and long forgotten. It is for me part of their charm.

LYMINGE
St. Mary and St. Ethelburga

No account of a visit to Lyminge parish church can do other than begin with Ethelburga, daughter of the founder of Canterbury and wife of Edwin of Northumbria, founder of York, for this church is redolent of her widowhood in Kent. After her husband was killed in battle in the North, she founded an abbey on the ruins of which this church is said to stand. A small plaque in the nave records the rule of Ethelburga and two other abbesses from 633 AD to 647 AD, followed by five abbots to 800 AD and finally priests, the last 'a secular priest, survivor of the Danish massacre in 850 AD'. Turbulent and violent times they were and we often forget how lucky we are today. Not far inland from Dover, Lyminge maintained its importance until the arrival of the Normans, for it was the centre of Limowart lathe, one of the seven administrative divisions of Saxon authority in Kent. It is understandable therefore that a substantial church should have replaced the abbey in the 10th century — presumably the Danes had added arson to murder in their catalogue of crimes in Kent.

Ethelburga, accordingly, is very much in one's mind as one looks at this church. It stands above its humdrum village on the western edge and is reached by passing under a flying buttress, added to prevent a slide downhill. To be fair, one should say that it is the village which has attached itself to the church and not the other way round. The walls, inside and out, are of old, uncovered rubblestone and, beside the porch at ground level, one can see a shallow recess in the south wall of the nave which, confusingly, once formed part of the north wall of Ethelburga's abbey and gave on to her tomb — at least that is how I read the literature. Apart from Ethelburga and the buttress flying over the churchyard path, the church is noteworthy for four small Saxon windows and the massive west tower, added in the 16th century. Curiously enough, as one looked at this tower, the higher up one's eye travelled the older it appeared. However, compared with the 10th century church and its Saxon windows with their Roman tiles for voussoirs, the tower is a parvenu.

Lyminge church must be the oldest, or at least one of the oldest churches that I have sketched in Kent. If one remembers its origins in the year 633 AD, it must qualify as the oldest and it cannot be altogether surprising to find Roman tiles here for, as the church leaflet observes, Ethelburga's foundation was only 250 years after the retreat of the legions to Rome. It bears its years lightly and, although the evidence of age is clear, there is not the slightest sign of neglect or dilapidation. The churchyard was trim and obviously cared for and the interior was spotless and full of Easter flowers. In the porch the notices were neatly headed in elegant italic script (having recently attended a weekend's introduction to the art of calligraphy, I can respect the skill and devotion that went into the preparation of these notices) and one can have little doubt that Ethelburga, Queen and Saint, would approve of the efforts of her present-day successors to preserve her church and memory.

* Limen was the Saxon name for Eastern Rother

ACRISE
Oak brushwood
St. Martin

If Lyminge is the oldest church in Kent so far explored by me, Acrise must surely rank as the spookiest. Totally invisible from the road, one approaches (on foot because the gate was padlocked) down a long drive between a dense screen of beech saplings and accompanied, in spring, by the incessant clamour of nesting rooks. At the end of the drive, cut off from the world of open prospects, one finds a claustrophobic little clearing in the midst of which stands the diminutive church. Around the clearing, or churchyard as it should more properly be termed, there is an untidy thicket of laurel bushes and miscellaneous trees partially concealing, on the south side, an immense Tudor/Victorian mansion complete with an equally grand stable block. This establishment, Acrise Place, came as a distinct shock to me; it seemed even more deserted and derelict than the church although manifestly the former has had its days of pride and pomp.

One might think that the church, so apparently isolated from everywhere, was built to be the private chapel of the great house but, with the evidence of Norman workmanship in the chancel walls (says Pevsner), St. Martin's arrived before the Papillons who built the first Place. Despite its close proximity to the mansion, this is a modest, unadorned little church consisting of a flint rendered nave and chancel plus a snug brick porch. Naturally enough, the door was locked and I assumed that the church's operational days were long over until I spied a notice setting out the roster of cleaning duties for the spring of 1985. The church door itself seemed even more incongruous than the red bricks of the porch against the Norman flintwork and Early English lancets of the chancel. Almost always the inner doorway of a porch, so far as I am aware, is contemporary with the wall of which it is part. Here the door is rectangular and panelled and looked to me as if it could have been a spare from Acrise Place. Unfortunately I could make out virtually nothing of the interior apart from the shapes of the balustrading of the gallery at the west end of the nave. The memorials inside refer, I gather, to the various occupants of Acrise Place; I sometimes wish, in these days of locked churches, that the practice of attaching memorial cartouches to the outside of the walls had been more prevalent. They never fail to embellish and add textual interest to the exterior.

My rough sketch beside the vestigial path to the Place was not prolonged; it did not seem imperative to linger and, if it had been twilight, I should have felt vaguely uneasy. To be honest I did anyway. There was an eerie atmosphere, heightened by notices around the perimeter proclaiming 'MOD – Out of Bounds to Troops'. To emphasise the point, near where I had parked my car the gates opening on to the park-like fields around were marked 'Gate to be kept shut unless Sentry posted'. What could it all mean? I half expected to see or hear skullduggery amongst the shadows; M.R. James, whose boyhood was spent in East Kent, must have known this church and perhaps it formed the inspiration for some of his haunting ghost stories.

There is no denying that Plaxtol village and its immediate neighbourhood are idyllic; it is the province of orchards and nut platts and winding lanes, still completely unspoilt by the 20th century. The church, at the head of the village street, commands the countryside and has a suitably severe and authoritative aspect. There is no suggestion of crumbling antiquity or softening in the cliff-like walls which confront one as one ascends the street. Indeed there cannot be, the church having been built as recently as 1649 but with much addition and enlargement in the second half of the last century. Until the Victorian 'improvements' this church counted as the one complete Cromwellian church in the county. Whether it is either the Reformation or the Victorian construction, the outward effect is the same; dressed ragstone blocks of uniform size, laid in regular courses and galleted throughout (for the benefit of those to whom galleting may be unfamiliar – it is the practice of inserting stone chips in the cement pointing between blocks). One occasionally sees it here and there in a church but, in my experience, never overall as at Plaxtol. Whoever was responsible here must have had galleting on the brain because it is extensively used in the wandering churchyard walls as well.

Basically the church consists of a west tower, chancel and nave with north and south transepts and north and south porches. It is the chancel, transepts and porches which are Victorian, nave and tower Cromwellian. There was once a gallery at the western end of the nave but this no longer exists, a loss leaving the wide nave with a barrackroom appearance, I think. The church is noteworthy for a hammerbeam roof and, certainly, the roof supports do distract one's attention from the bare, whitewashed walls. Two features stand out in a somewhat featureless, puritan interior – an immense organ entirely filling the north transept (perhaps it would have been preferable to retain the musicians' gallery) and the matching set of embroidered hassocks which impress one as of the fruits of a cottage industry from the village.

When it comes to artistic composition, Plaxtol church is obstinately uncooperative. Immediately below the church to the south and east the narrow road curves round and, if I had wanted a view from that direction, I should have had to establish myself in one of the bedrooms of the facing cottages or, further off, in the park of Fairlawne House – neither alternative a practical proposition. To the north and north west lies the irregular churchyard, well stocked with spreading yews to block a composition, but, in compensation, generously endowed with early tombstones. As I understand it, tombstones only came into use about 1700 so it gave me considerable satisfaction to sit with my back to two dated 1737 and 1762 with three others of similar age close by. Everywhere there are others, carved and decorated, mine having a convincingly realistic skull above the inscription. In the porch there lay a miniature dated 1643 (unless my eyes deceived me) – prior to the building of the church! – taken, I imagine, from the ranks of its fellows which line the foot of the churchyard walls. If one wished to summarise Plaxtol church, one might describe it as sparse within, profuse without.

Fordwich on the Stour, close to the east of Canterbury and once its port but with its working days long completed, has resisted pretty well the march of progress while reaching that dangerous condition of beauty spot. As a magnet for tourists, of whom in honesty I cannot exclude myself, the little church must play a not insignificant part. It stands at the heart of the village and should best be viewed, I suspect, from the opposite bank below the bridge.

It is a dear little church, dating mainly from the 13th century although traces of the outline of a Saxon doorway above a small side door at the foot of the tower suggest a church here as early as the 7th century, claims the church pamphlet. The walls are a happy blend of uncoursed, rough ragstone blocks, flint and mortar, reinforced by substantial buttresses. Presumably the latter were added after the floods in the 1200s had attacked the foundations and caused the church to list – a fact that is still evident today. Surprisingly in the circumstances but in conformity with the theory of the stability of structures, there are no buttresses to the tower. It has, as you see, a spire with four little spirelights on the cardinal faces and this extra weight and thrust would seem to me to call for lateral support. Still there it all is, surviving from the 7th or 13th centuries and that is a long time and an endurance test for any structure.

The visitor is encouraged to enter and rewarded by what he finds. First there are the solid but leaning, rectangular piers, cut from the original nave wall and which now separate the nave from the north aisle; then there is the unspoilt pre-Victorian paved floor, the unrestored box pews and the windows framed by their unplastered stone surrounds. More important than these permanent fixtures, I would judge, must be the enigmatic length of carved stone, said to be a fragment of a Norman stone tomb, or alternatively, to be taken from the tomb of St Augustine. Perhaps the latter theory is now discounted for the stone is here at Fordwich and not at Canterbury where it lay briefly after a sojourn in Fordwich churchyard. One wishes it could speak and set the speculations at rest. Beside it in the aisle stands something even more primitive – a decidedly uncomfortable, stiff-backed stool cut from a single piece of tree trunk. Its age and origin are unknown but one suggestion is that it came ashore from a raiding Viking longship; another supposition is that it was a 'penitent's chair' used for erring women in the Middle Ages. What was the male equivalent – stocks?

Fordwich church is now very compactly encased in its period village, barely a stone's throw from the 15th century 'town hall' – a competing tourist attraction. Along with many others I had lunch in the pub on the quay facing this civic relic. It is worth noting, with relief so far as I was concerned but probably with regret by some, that none of these visitors entered the church while I was in it nor disturbed me as I sat on the bank of cow parsley to make my sketch. What a blessing for Fordwich church (to my unsociable mind) that there is a rival attraction to distract the passing crowd.

Like its near neighbour Fordwich, Sturry was also a port on the Stour for Canterbury. That sounds bustling and commercial, as no doubt it was, but in the days when the Jutes settled here and later when the Danes raided and wintered in Kent, the Stour was tidal upriver as far almost as Canterbury and both Sturry and Fordwich must have been convenient berthing and unloading places. Fordwich in fact was important enough to have a mayor and return an MP for Parliament – I don't know if Sturry can match that claim but probably not as Arthur Mee makes no mention of such glories. The sea has long receded; Fordwich is a backwater now but Sturry is still a highway – for road traffic, regrettably, which must make this village a purgatory for those who live beside the road to Thanet. Poor Sturry; if ever there was a case for a by-pass, this old beached port must be one.

Wisely, or luckily, the church is set well back from the traffic, separated by a broad, tree-lined sweep of grass, neglected now and the playground of wind-blown scraps of paper. Sensibly the people of Sturry prefer to keep to the north side, under the lee of the church, in all their commerce with St. Nicholas. Indeed, this must have always been the case, even before the traffic became so unsupportable, for towards the main road the churchyard is untidy and bereft of headstones; to the north all is tranquil, congested with tombstones and just as a churchyard should be. Churches have always been places of sanctuary – here at Sturry the building acts as a bulwark against the tides of the 20th century as well.

The church is a good strong rubblestone and flint building of many centuries in provenance – Norman to start with, Perpendicular in the main and 19th century for the porch. There is a fine west tower, a nave and aisles, chancel and chapel. Pevsner says the tower is Norman and remarks on its idiosyncratic steeped buttresses which strongly resemble those of Brook church. They are so distinctive that I would think that both towers could be the work of the same master mason. The churchyard notice-board proclaimed that the church serves both the Anglican and Methodist persuasions. Despite this ecumenical display the church was locked, to the extent that the handle of the porch's outer door had been removed.

My sketch scarcely does justice to the almost hidden church. In default of an entry, I was compensated by the Tudor brick wall that separates the churchyard from ground which was successively monks' grange, country retreat of an ex-colonial pro-consul, and now the appendix to a boys' public school. There is a grand Tudor gateway giving access to the grassy drive in which I sat, sadly out of the scope of my vision, but the mellow churchyard gateway and the pleached trees served well enough for a composition even if they are largely at the expense of the object of my visit, the Norman successor to a Saxon chapel.

NEWENDEN
St. Peter

At the new woodland pasture

This is an oddly attractive little sandstone church. It is perched abruptly above the road to Rye before it crosses the Rother at what was once the lowest crossing of the river and this accident of geography may explain why the Romans chose this place for their city of Anderida, or so it is said. After their departure, Hengist the Saxon made a brief end of habitation here when he put every last individual to the sword in 488AD; but the earthworks of the early Britons remain and settlement returned (vide a royal charter from Offa, king of Mercia). Now the Rother has altered its course, the sea receded and the geographical importance of Newenden diminished to extinction, a change that I am sure is welcomed by the two hundred or so parishioners today. Still the church survives, as have churches all over Kent, despite the ravages of time.

It stands so close to the busy road that it comes as a bit of a shock when suddenly encountered point-blank. It looks like a vestige, which is what it is, with a huge roof reaching almost to ground level on either side. In 1985 it is but a mutilated fragment of what stood before and this can be deduced from the broken stump of wall protruding from where the nave is joined by the chancel on the south side and, more dramatically, at the equivalent point on the north side by the exposure, low down, of a foot or two of octagonal column which must have formed part of a grand arcade or chancel arch.

And this brings one to the chancel itself. As one comes into the church and looks down the foreshortened nave one is, at first sight, confronted by a semi-circular Norman arch shielding the darkened privacy of the secretive chancel beyond. The reality is a happy surprise for this diminutive neo-Norman chancel was built in 1930 to commemorate the memory of sixteen people whose names are carved on the priest's doorway. The reason for the new chancel, and also for the endearingly self-important Victorian bell tower, was general collapse at the end of the 17th century which left no more than the nave and north aisle to remind us of former glories. Newenden church is more fortunate than most in its recent replacements; in their separate ways they have both added charm to an unusual village church and make it well worth more than a passing inspection.

Some might say that the church is most notable as the repository for its Norman font. Fonts tend to outlast churches and Newenden's pride is a magnificent specimen, both in size and decoration, and would not look out of place in a cathedral. It is a substantial square block carved on three sides, with animals on two, pomegranates on the third. There must be some significance to these fruit; they are not particularly edible but, with their spiky crowns, they look absolutely gorgeous in the natural state. Why should pomegranates appear on the font? Could it be an association of seeds with the sacrament of baptism — the birth of religious life? If so, their representation on a font seems more appropriate than the savage creatures depicted on the other panels.

ROLVENDEN
St. Mary the Virgin

After a morning spent at Newenden, Rolvenden's church seemed like St. Paul's cathedral, even to the extent of the revolving doorway at the base of the tower. It is a spacious church set in an equally capacious churchyard overlooking the road that runs through the village. Betjeman in his 'Pocket Guide to English Parish Churches' says that it is best approached from the east and no doubt he is right. From that direction, amongst the tombstones, one is rewarded by the three gable ends of the chancel and the flanking chapels with their handsome Perpendicular windows and with a vista of receding tiled roofs culminating in the west tower. To have attempted a sketch à la Betjeman I would have had to forego the full, dramatic effect of the tall, dark, ironstone tower framed by the period cottages leading past the war memorial. The tower won; it was built in the Decorated style and accordingly takes precedence. This must also be the picture of the church that springs most readily to mind of all except those who explore the further recesses of the churchyard – a second argument in favour of the western front.

Inside, two aisles and lofty ceilings confirm the general air of spaciousness. It is essentially a church of the Decorated period later enlarged in the Perpendicular style by wealthy patrons up to the year 1470 when all construction here ceased for good – more or less coincident with the crisis of the Wars of the Roses. I do not know if there is any significance in that fact but major dynastic upheavals must have discouraged the private plans of many great landlords. Interior improvement, however, was not affected and did continue so that, now, one of the most interesting features of this church is a pair of squire's pews. In the north chapel we have the pew of the Monypenny family (who incidentally in recent years provided a succession of vicars here at Hadlow), christened locally as the 'dining room pew' and to balance it, in the south chapel, the 'drawing room pew'. The latter is elevated above the chapel floor (reserved for the servants) and reached by an elegant curved staircase and furnished with a table and a set of Sheraton chairs. This pew was the preserve of the Gybbon family and, I suppose, apart from local standing, their claim to fame must rest on a cousinly relationship with the author of the 'Decline and Fall'. Both pews are anachronisms but delightful relics of past privilege and are rightly cherished at Rolvenden.

On a much more sombre note, this church records the death by martyrdom at the stake in Canterbury in 1555 of John Frankish, vicar here, and three others for the heretical crime of denying the doctrine of transubstantiation. Almost as painful to record, Frankish was shopped by the vicar of Tenterden. I wonder what the victims would have to say to their successors in the Church today. To end, though, more cheerfully, I found the use of a chancel buttress to memorialise the early death of a twenty five year old wife of 1770 far more civilised, Christian and heartwarming in temper than the sad Rolvenden history of Maryan persecution two centuries before.

HORSMONDEN　　　　　　　　　　　　　　　　　*Horse stream pasture*
St. Margaret

On the first occasion that I saw this church, I attempted a view of the tower from the west, amongst the hop poles. It was hardly a success as I was soon interrupted by an officious foreman. However my ruffled feelings were considerably soothed by the least likely of the workers there who later took the trouble to apologise for his superior. This time I decided not to offend among the hop poles and to stick to the churchyard. Here I encountered an aimiable lady busy spraying weedkiller on the nettles. She informed me of the 'exploded myth' that the unoccupied section of the churchyard had been a plague burial ground, a claim that could be substantiated by the absent village. She also mentioned a reputed Saxon tomb in the south chapel, now vestry cum organ loft. I could find no trace of a tomb and since neither Pevsner nor the church pamphlet list a Saxon tomb, one must reluctantly class this legend with that of the plague burial as doubtful.

This is a grand church, the more so in view of its isolation in the fields. It is essentially the creation of the second rector, Henry de Grofhurst, who inspired the building at the start of the 14th century. Despite the Black Death, it was complete by the end of the century and has endured basically the same ever since. The founding father is now rightly famous as well for his portrait in brass on the chancel floor. Later the church became the virtual fief of the Smith-Marriott family who presided as patrons and vicars for a remarkable span from 1785 to 1944. In their care of their church this family is convincing argument for nepotism.

To come to the church, it is built of honey-coloured ashlared sandstone. There is a nice little wooden porch, contemporary with the church, ('open night and day' claimed my lady informant); a wide uncluttered nave, north and south aisles, south chapel and, of course, the four-square west tower. Not surprisingly most of the memorials are those of the Smith-Marriott family but one could not help noticing the bust of the inventor in 1923 of the unromantic but worthy stomach pump. In the fabric the church still possesses two claustrophobic stone staircases to rood lofts so presumably there have been screens in different positions at different times. The pews in the nave rest comfortably on honest stone flags but, in the chancel and vestry, Victorian tiles less aesthetically hold the floor − mercifully hidden by wall to wall carpeting; an excellent answer to encaustic vitreous tiles. All things considered the church looked to be in first-class condition so I was a little surprised to read that that admirable society, The Friends of Kent Churches, are currently contributing to repairs. Removal of that intrusive organ from the south chapel would be my recommendation.

Instead of a sketch from the hopfield, shown here is a view from the east. Just as pictorial, really, but as my churchyard acquaintance observed, few would recognise it as a portrait of Horsmonden. A similar stricture might be applied to all too many of my sketches but once in this little book they are at least identified by text.

JAS

ST. MARY-IN-THE-MARSH
St. Mary the Virgin

On a slight knoll and encircled by a stout, oaken rail and post fence, St. Mary the Virgin stands at a crossroads in the heart of Romney Marsh where the sheep outnumber humans by one hundred to one, or even five hundred to one. With its solid, three-stage, Norman tower and long, undifferentiated nave and chancel roof, supported by the roofs of its miniature aisles, the church might be compared, not altogether fancifully, to an upturned trimaran, tethered to its mooring post against the onslaughts of wind and weather. When the first parts of the church were built in the early days of the 12th century I imagine that the protecting sea wall of the Marsh was not what it is today and the menace of the sea more immediate, so my nautical fancies need not be entirely irrelevant; indeed they seem to be corroborated by the inner door of the porch which can only be described as 'clinker built', as are most run-of-the-mill small boats.

Inside, the sea vanishes and one is confronted by a light, airy and unspoilt church. This impression derives, I think, from the absence of any arch separating chancel and nave and from the rafters of the roof which appear to have been scraped clean and are certainly less sombre than is usually the case. The floor is an expanse of matt, brick-red tiles enlivened here and there by a grave old ledger stone – exactly what one would welcome in any church. Above are the unrestored box pews, which are nice, but it would be even better if the original high white box pews could have been retained. Worm and decay, I expect, were the cause of the replacement. There is no bulky, obstructive organ; just a modest harmonium and, for this relief from a piece of furniture which was inconceivable when these churches were laid out, one can only feel grateful. More appropriate to its antiquity are the recessed sedilia in the chancel wall. Here was stone seating for the celebrants of the services; most uncomfortable they look for there cannot be as much as one foot between floor and seat but perhaps the chancel floor has since been raised. Framing the sedilia is a hood mould (against the falling rain?) stopped by a stone corbel at each end. One is the head of a tonsured monk, the other an imp with bared teeth; a balancing of good and evil which might be taken as a medieval precedent for the BBC's habit of giving equal weight to the right and left wing politics of the 20th century.

Sedilia apart, this church is noteworthy for the presence of a simple memorial in the churchyard to the authoress E. Nesbit. Her grave is marked by an unpretentious wooden rail and post arrangement which hardly reflects her fame in life but without a doubt it is by her books for children that she will be best remembered.

My view of the ragstone tower and its irregular, lop-sided buttresses, to the regretted exclusion of the body of the church, was dictated by the necessity, in my opinion, of avoiding two flowering cherries. Decorative as these ornamental trees may be, they do seem more suited to the garden paths of suburban villas than to that of a windswept church in the remoter reaches of Romney Marsh.

SNAVE
St. Augustine

The name of the stream nearby

To the passing, uninformed observer like myself, Snave church is a distinct conundrum. It stands, miles from anywhere in Romney Marsh, accompanied only by three post-Victorian houses and nibbling sheep. Why, for a start, is it where it is and why is there no trace of anything remotely contemporary to justify its presence?

It is an old church of square west tower, nave, chancel and north chapel, by no means insignificant in dimensions. Externally, Pevsner dates it as fourteen some-thing; internally as twelve something. He says the external details are 'suspect'; presumably because his datings conflict; Arthur Mee ignores this church entirely – an unusual oversight for him – so does Betjeman. But not me.

It was restored in 1873 – for what purpose? There is scaffolding round the tower today (May 1985) and severe notices in the churchyard saying 'Warning. Danger of Falling Stones. Keep Away'. The tower has obviously had some attention lately for the old rubble ragstone is almost submerged under an unsightly coat of cement pointing. A great pity. The doorway at the foot of the tower, with its two obliterated corbel heads, looks untouched but the door has a modern yale lock; although locked and unused in appearance, this doorway must be the entrance to the church for the south porch is like no other porch that I have seen. Ignored by the restorers of 1873 and disregarded today, there is now no roof, only rafters; the side walls are partly collapsed and a healthy elderberry monopolises the strewn interior while a semi-prostrate laburnum leans protectively towards the skeleton of the entrance. Why has the porch been so abandoned and the tower so defaced in the pursuit of protection?

In contrast, the surroundings are neat and trim. One approaches from the road down a wide, grassy drive, past two well-found farm gates to a pleasant churchyard, fenced with oak and fringed about by a regular cordon of mature maples and chest-nuts. The grass is not long (the sheep very likely) and the gravestones not overgrown or unduly dilapidated. Why so cared for and how can anyone plaster a medieval tower with cement and yet watch a porch disintegrate? It is all such an odd contrast – scaffolding here, roofless rafters there and it is not as if the porch has only recently deteriorated. Clearly its demise has been going on for a long time.

I cannot comment on the interior. Seen opaquely through the accessible windows, there appeared to be an altar in the chancel and pews in the nave. There are also sedilia, says Pevsner, 'embattled', no less. In a different sense, the whole church looks embattled and one would like to know the outcome. Will it survive to be used and who will use it in this empty marsh; will the scaffolding come down and the tower, with its 'falling stones' stay up or will it slowly go the way of the porch?* With no-one there to explain, this lonely church has some of that teasing fascination which the silent monuments of the past so often have.

* I have since learnt that Snave has indeed been declared redundant and only just escaped an even worse fate.

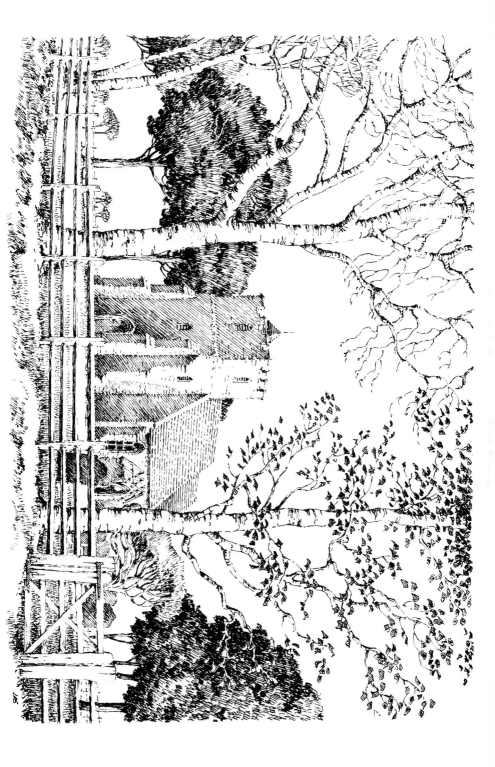

This is a fascinating church, contemporary with Lyminge to the east and very similar in origin for it, also, is based on a nunnery founded by a widowed Saxon queen, who like her mother-in-law went on to be canonised. The surviving traces of the nunnery are here more conspicuous and give this church, or more properly abbey, such a distinctive flavour. Essentially it consists of a Norman north aisle and chapel, incorporating what remains from the nunnery after the Danes had left their destructive mark, to which has been added, in the 13th century, a parish church of nave and chancel. It is this juncture of one old church with another that gives Sheppey's minster its remarkable double-barrelled appearance. All that remained was to add a west tower for the bells; here they seem to have left things a trifle late for the dissolution of the monastries in Henry VIII's reign interrupted construction so that the ambitious stone tower was terminated in a wooden belfry two thirds of the way up.

Inside, one's interest inevitably concentrates on the Saxo-Norman north half. My arrival coincided with the end of a service and there were several people about, one of whom helpfully attached herself to me and announced herself as a 'guide'. Certainly, without her local knowledge, I should never have noticed the tiny quatrefoil aperture in the wall of the nun's chapel which my guide asserted was there to show that the chapel had been sited on pagan ground. It does not seem convincing but there are Roman tiles in the walls and there was a temple here. The walls of this chapel contain vestiges of blocked openings which suggest that the Norman layout differs to some extent from that known to the Saxon nuns. I found it incongruous that the latter should have used, for the corbel stone of a low doorway arch, the head of a man putting out his tongue; as a decoration it hardly shows the refinement that one expects of a nunnery devoted to good works and helping the poor.

Minster must also be renowned for the splendid recumbent stone figures of knights interred within. There are four of these; one is held to be either the Duke of Clarence (he of the butt of malmsey wine) or Lord Badlesmere. The latter, a grandee of Kent, seems more likely but it would be interesting to know if either was particularly tall in life as this figure seems to me to be unusually elongated. Another effigy is that of an unknown resurrected from the churchyard, a third that of the power of the day in Sheppey, de Shurland. The last crowns the elaborate free-standing tomb of Henry VIII's treasurer, Sir Thomas Cheyne. It is a distinguished quartet and obviously attracts considerable attention and local pride for the tombs are all generously scored with the initials of later generations.

When accepted by Sexburga for her foundation, this must have been a marvellous site. It is the high point of Sheppey and commands sweeping views over the Thames estuary on one side and the Swale channel and North Kent on the other. Ignore the uninspiring modern buildings and, even today, one's eye is transported. In the days of the Saxon nuns it was the Danes who were the desecrators; in this century it has been ourselves.

EASTCHURCH
All Saints

Whoever designed this church must have had a geometrical fixation, or so the church's portable information board suggests. To be numerate in my turn, I learnt that the width of the nave equals the sum of the width of the two aisles; the width of the nave plus aisles equals the length of the nave; and the width of the aisles equals the height of the capitals of the arcade pillars. I should not have been aware of these pleasing equations unprompted but certainly the proportions are agreeable and may probably conform to some architectural canon of the 1400s, the Perpendicular period, when this church was built. Very likely many other churches follow similar conventions in layout — one just has not had the wit to realise it unaided.

Considering its sadly plain village, this is an elaborate church. The nave, chancel, aisles, porches and tower are all castellated, banded with flint and, in the case of the tower, chequered; very impressive it all looks as, no doubt, it was meant to. One criticism I must make, levelled against the Victorian restorers: bearing in mind its age, five hundred years plus, the ragstone fabric should look wonderful, mellowed and softened by all those summers and winters of sunshine and rain. But the genial effects of the weather are overridden, as is often the case, I am afraid, by unduly prominent and unsympathetic pointing; the method used here is, I believe, called 'ribbon pointing' — very effective from a builder's point of view. I daresay, but disaster from an aesthetic standpoint.

Inside one can forget the good but misguided intentions of the preservationists and concentrate on the dimensions. Here the numbers game is repeated in the roof where eighteen carved angels, clasping armorial shields, act as corbels for the rafters and nine further angels, with outspread wings, gaze down from the central bosses. Eastchurch undoubtedly possesses one of the better roofs that I have seen in Kent. To match the angels above, the complete rood screen remains intact — all forty six feet of it; like the angels, a multiple of nine, give or take one foot. Beyond the impenetrable screen one can glimpse a memorial which includes, as a 'weeper', the figure of a young man who grew up to sign the death warrant of Charles I. Perhaps that is why the screen is kept locked and bolted.

Sheppey is lucky to have two such outstanding churches as the Minster and Eastchurch; it has been a forgotten island, avoided by the gentry and somewhat deprived in consequence. Now largely given over to fossils, wildfowl and holiday camps on the coastline, sheep in the marshes (Sheppey — sheep island) and, less welcome, a prison in the centre, the island has not prospered. However, change is not everywhere resisted and the replacement of the obsolete naval dockyard at Sheerness by a modern roll-on, roll-off ferry port bids fair to transform the island from obscurity to affluence. In due course the surroundings of the Minster and Eastchurch must recover and all those battlements, angels and recumbent knights may then enjoy a setting which they more properly deserve. Here, at least, there is promise of a better future.

BRENCHLEY
All Saints

Braenci's clearing

Very few churches in Kent, or anywhere else for that matter, can have a church-yard path to compare with Brenchley's. My sketch was made from the north east corner of the churchyard, beside the path, and, apart from a clutter of 19th century bodystones, majors almost exclusively on the magnificent topiary yews which line the path from the lychgate to the porch. There are ten of these, close planted, virtually uniform in shape and roughly twenty five feet in height; estimated by the church pamphlet to be nearly four hundred years old. For anyone with a naval background they must remind him or her of the custom of making an arch of swords beneath which the bride and bridegroom pass on leaving the church. Here they dominate a hillside church which in its turn has been the dominant feature of its village for seven hundred years.

Next in visual importance after the yews must come the turret-capped tower which Pevsner describes as 'handsome at a distance, less satisfactory at a close inspection'. That, I think, might not be the opinion of the ordinary mortal; it looks as confident and impressive when glimpsed towering above the yews as it does when seen from the base of the massive buttresses. The church is built on the south slope of the hill which descends to the wandering Teise rivulet and settlement could always have been a problem. That might explain the enormous buttresses which support the tower from all quarters, including those inside the nave, and for the evident make and mend in-filling of ragstone in the softer golden sandstone. Two amiable and informative masons, who had been renewing the pointing, told me that the chancel has been coming away from one of its northern buttresses. As the buttress would not be climbing up the hill, it follows that the church is still tending downhill. However it has been where it is for so long that the rate of movement must be minimal. As to the pointing, I was relieved when the masons agreed that unsympathetic pointing on the walls outside could be as destructive of ancient virtue as are Victorian vitreous tiles on the floors within; the work on the offending buttress was commendably inconspicuous.

It was while examining the pointing that I had a close encounter with a pair of swifts. For a few minutes I watched in admiration as they darted, backwards and forwards past my nose, to their nest under the eaves, occasionally emitting their shrill screams. They are marvellously aerobatic and a part of the summer atmos-phere of country churches. I was riveted.

The interior of the church does not quite live up to the exterior, I think (others would disagree I am sure), notwithstanding several highly rated memorials. These commemorate the long-departed members of local families, worthy no doubt in their day and sure enough of themselves to secure a place in the church but none of sufficient historical importance to stir the imagination. Brenchley was also, I gather, the parish church for the neighbouring villages of Paddock Wood and Matfield, a plurality that may account for the lack of identifying character in these two less fortunate villages. No village is complete without its medieval church and Brenchley's is good enough for three.

PATRIXBOURNE
St. Mary

A remarkable little church about which much is written by the experts. For the non-expert it is difficult to avoid superficial banalities – however I will try.

To begin with my sketch, although it includes all the external essentials except one, it conveys little or no impression of the charming churchyard and vintage village. My architectural omission is a circular 'wheel' window high in the east wall of the chancel – a 'rare glory' (Pevsner). Not omitted but impossible to portray adequately in a small sketch are the Norman doorways. If Ruskin had passed this way (instead of gallivanting around Italy) I am sure he would have written, and illustrated, whole chapters about these entrances. They are outstanding examples of the stonemason's art and it is remarkable that they have defied the elements for eight hundred years without obliteration. My attempts to describe these carved stones are prudently limited to saying that the door under the tower has five semi-circular bands of decoration forming the voussoirs and a niche above for the guardian angel. Similarly, above the priest's door to the right there is a time-worn figure, thought to be that of St. Thomas à Becket whose murder more or less coincided with the foundation of this church. There is also, framing the tower doorway, a canopy outline in the shape of a gable; it looks as if a roofed porch once protected the doorway but the decorations on the stone belie this theory. It is certainly unusual.

The church owes much to its benefactors who lived in the great house alongside, now demolished. In 1855 the Norman tower was restored by the Marchioness Conyngham, vide the unblemished Caen quoin stones holding together the old rubble and flint walling. (It is not known to me when the top-heavy spire was added, but I do know that it was reshingled in 1954 at a cost of £750; ours at Hadlow, smaller in size, was reshingled in 1984 at a cost of thousands!) In 1876, the Marquis Conyngham presented the tower clock; it is quite inconspicuous and, if one had arrived from Mars, say, with no knowledge of the earthly past, one might well assume that the clock and tower were both of the same period. Full marks to the Marquis.

Inside, one is surprised at how small and cluttered the church seems in relation to the dominant tower – possibly because the layout includes the base of the tower within the south aisle. Chiefly memorable is the stained glass which delights the connoisseurs. Not being one, I will simply mention its existence to square my yardarm with the purists and pass on to other things. There are of course many memorials to the Conyngham family and their predecessors at the manor. One luxury they once enjoyed was an open fireplace in the private chapel. Now gone – and with it a small reminder of past privilege. A loss for the antiquarian.

Described by the late John Betjeman as a 'unique example of Norman architecture', Patrixbourne must surely appear in any listing of the parish churches of England, on account of its Norman doorways, if nothing else. I would include it for its harmonious clock face and for the nine scratch dials that I counted on the pillars of the doorway.

Bekesbourne must live, I think, rather in the shadow of its more famous neighbour, Patrixbourne. Reached down a lane off a minor road, across a splash of the Nailbourne stream and up through a cherry orchard, the church is remote and not easy to find. Indeed, I was so disorientated on arrival it seemed as if the tower was at the east end, the chancel at the west. All of which makes Bekesbourne a very suitable place of refuge, which it became, but, more surprisingly considering the Nailbourne is liable to dry in summer, a 'limb' of a Cinque port — namely Hastings. I gather though that this privilege was more the product of ownership than a phenomenon of geography.

The church, on the top of its hill, is a longish but low, straight-forward, flint construction of nave and chancel with a rebuilt tower plus an 18th century transept on the unfrequented south side. Pevsner says that this addition is faced with the earliest example in Kent of mathematical tiles; I found it somewhat nondescript but then I find mathematical tiles a bit bogus. The architectural interest here, as at Patrixbourne, is the Norman doorway on the north side with its semi-circular orders of intricate moulding. The rest of the flinty exterior is so regular that I reluctantly had to concentrate my sketch on this doorway, with all the attendant difficulties of reproduction.

Not unexpectedly the church was locked but it was my good fortune to time my departure with the arrival of one of the volunteer ladies who look after the interior so I gratefully followed her in. It is rather dark inside, the nave walls being unplastered flints — attractive notwithstanding. With little scope for elaboration, the layout here makes the most of the limited space available. For instance, the organ, always an intrusion, has been neatly accommodated in the transept, rather as in a built-in cupboard, and the rood screen has been moved from its proper position between nave and chancel to the west end of the nave where it forms a small vestry — a far better solution than the destruction of the screen. Of memorials, the principal one, a hanging effigy of a kneeling figure in armour, was moved to the base of the tower from its original position; I suppose its weight was too much for the unreinforced flint walls. (I often wonder how the Italians manage it, for many of their church walls, although made of brick, apparently effortlessly support huge stone sarcophagi well clear of the ground. They must have some hidden counterweight which a simple structure like that at Bekesbourne could not possibly provide.)

There is a handsome pulpit, with sounding board above; too recent however for Archbishop Thomas Cranmer's use when he preached here. If was after the death of his patron, Henry VIII, and the accession of Mary, with his future menacingly threatened, that he took refuge in his palace across the stream. He was not permitted to linger in peace or retirement at Bekesbourne but, before he was taken away he hid his will in the palace where it remained until found one hundred years later by marauding Roundheads. I cannot see the point of hiding a will; I fear that the poor archbishop must have suffered in his life from unsound testamentary advice as well as political misfortune.

BISHOPSBOURNE
St. Mary and St. Nicholas

Self evident

Bishopsbourne is the merest hamlet, untroubled now by the 20th century. All it seems to consist of is three or four handsome houses, some pretty cottages, a cosy pub, parklike fields around and, of course, a medieval church. It is the sort of place one would like to live in oneself and one unconsciously keeps an eye open for 'For Sale' notices; naturally there were none.

Apparently there was a church here before the coming of the Normans but the present building is 13th century with later additions. The walls are of uncoursed, knapped flints, partly rendered and over-repointed by the zealous Victorians. It consists of a nave flanked by narrow aisles, a chancel balanced by two small chapels and a massive, impressive (but not to Pevsner who describes it as 'unimpressive') Perpendicular west tower — one of the later additions, no doubt. This tower is distinguished from most others I have drawn by the suppression of the stair turret within the angle of the south west buttress — only revealed externally by the segment of tiling halfway up.

One enters the church through a small north doorway (no porch) and steps down into the aisle, as is so often the case. One would, I think, expect to step up into a church but, in some curious way, medieval churches tend to settle comfortably into the ground and churchyards to rise up around them. No commentary on Bishopsbourne can ignore the south chapel where generations of one family are recorded on the walls and on the 16th century stained-glass window; or the stained-glass window in the tower by Burne-Jones; or fail to mention the barely discernible traces of wall painting above the arches of the nave. Much more obvious, incongruous even, is the deep skirting of mosaic tiling which gives the chancel a somewhat Islamic appearance. Unusual, too, is the small window above the tower arch designed, I imagine, to perform a similar function to that of a squint in a chancel arch — for a bellringer perhaps.

Bishopsbourne is celebrated for, or congratulates itself on, two rectors (newcomers to me, I must confess), namely Richard Hooker, who compiled eight volumes of a legalistic defence of the English Church at the Reformation, and Joseph Reade FRS, as much an amateur scientist as a Victorian divine. Joseph Conrad also lived in the house alongside the church so obviously Bishopsbourne has not simply been a backwater of rustic innocence. Quite the reverse in fact; the living has been a promotion prospect as the list of vicars makes clear. Here we find that, since records began in 1280, the vicars have obtained two archbishoprics, ten bishoprics, seven archdeaconries, four deaneries, four canonries, a chancellorship of Cambridge and a Mastership of the Temple (Hooker); a remarkable record of achievement for a country living. Could the explanation be that Canterbury is only a few miles away and that more time was spent politicking there than in preaching in the delightful valley of the Nailbourne. I know which I would rather do but Bishopsbourne has every reason to feel proud of its past incumbents.

Writing about Barham, Kingston's neighbouring village two miles upstream on the Nailbourne, Arthur Mee quotes this strip of Kent as 'the most historic mile of countryside in England'. I do not know whether this famous mile includes Kingston because today it is utterly peaceful and withdrawn. One would never guess that on the Downs near here Caesar's legions camped, fought and routed the Britons or that King John and Simon de Montfort both camped hereabouts with their armies for different reasons and in different reigns but on occasions of great consequence for each of them and for their followers. Any wounds inflicted then have long since healed.

Kingston's present ease is no longer disturbed by great events and one now finds a small, compact, untroubled village with the church on its raised churchyard above the clustered houses. There is no lychgate but the road winds round a good retaining wall before coming to a dead end beyond which the fields ascend to the Downs above. The church is old and simple – just a chancel, facing you as you approach up the path, an aisleless nave, a north porch and a Perpendicular west tower; all on a modest scale as befits a church that originated in the 11th century, never progressed to much enlargement or aggrandisement, and has always been, I expect, overshadowed by its next-door neighbours, Bishopsbourne and Barham. From what one can see from the outside, if the weather vane is anything to go by, the orientation of Kingston deviates from the east/west axis by some ten degrees – not that that matters. It is also evident that the fabric has been deteriorating for some time as the flint walling has been extensively covered by stucco and, in the case of the chancel, by what looks suspiciously like pebble dash. Indeed there seems to have been even more fundamental reconstruction to the chancel; here the east window cannot be more than two hundred years old whereas it should be at least as old and emaciated as the other windows of the chancel. The original must be elsewhere and my explanation would be that it, or rather the curved remnants of its arch, now acts as the framework for the garden gate of the old rectory. This is only the second time that I have seen use made of redundant masonry – the first was at Hartlip near Sittingbourne where the medieval doorway frames one of the churchyard gateways. In principle, I would far rather see the original stonework preserved in its proper place, reinforced by iron staples if necessary, but if it has to be replaced, I am all for its ornamental use elsewhere, as in this gateway. It must always be a pleasure to pass beneath old stones that have seen seven or more centuries elapse. I envy the old rectory its gateway.

The church door was locked, understandably perhaps as the church is said to contain a complete suit of armour (eminently collectable) and a seven hundred year old font which was once extracted to do duty as a cattle trough (Arthur Mee). Seen through the windows, the nave looked neat and trim but relatively unadorned. If one could have seen into the chancel one might have observed the carved angels in the roof above and the kneeling knight on the floor below.

BILSINGTON
St. Peter and St. Paul

Bilswid's farmstead

One would think that Bilsington, an inconspicuous hamlet on the fringe of Romney Marsh, must owe its existence to the priory established there in 1253 by a magnate who was not only Chief Justice, but also Keeper of the Great Seal, Lord Warden of the Cinque Ports, Provost of Beverley and chaplain to Henry III – a pillar, if not a bastion, of the establishment one might say. One might also suppose that the church, a mile away and now cunningly hidden by a moated farm, followed the priory, but I feel it may have been the other way round if the blocked Norman window above the porch is anything to go by. When my wife and I arrived here, seven hundred years later, we found a large gathering of mothers, children and cars below the churchyard picking strawberries and picnicking – a splendid way to combine a day out in the sun in the boundless marshland fields with earning a little pin money.

The church is a distinctly simple structure of nave, no aisles, chancel and tower – once appropriated to the priory but from the dissolution of the monasteries standing on its own feet, or footings. It was in 1590 that the tower was added, or so it is dated in stone. That would be after the church's separation from the priory and may explain its abbreviated appearance. It is as if ambition overreached resources – constructed of stone for half the way up then only a truncated shingled belfry capped by the briefest of spirelets. Oddly attractive it all looks today. In their belated drive for economy, the builders seem to have miscalculated, though, over that bell in the foreground. It weighs over nine hundredweight and must have proved more than the tower could bear, hence its installation on the ground. It was cast in the 15th century (before the tower was built – perhaps it came from the priory) and was paid for by a 'fishmonger of London', and of Bilsington too, no doubt. It is a ponderous bell and one wonders how they managed to cart it down here without accident from Whitechapel where most bells seem to have been cast. There must have been a few crossed fingers and Ave Marias en route.

Inside, the church is rather bare and clinical – one might have thought little used, but the vases of summer flowers contradicted such an unworthy suspicion. To brighten the austerity there is a particularly florid example of the statutory royal coat of arms, those of George III, and a neat hatchment of a Lord Justice. What was, or is, remarkable was a large sheet of paper pinned to the vestry screen on which an attempt is being made to plot the layout of the graves in the churchyard. Rows of names are already shown, many more than there are headstones, and it makes one realise how many people must lie below the grass on which one so carelessly wanders when one visits a church. The completed diagram may never exactly represent the truth, but it could be more permanent and informative than indecipherable tombstones or anonymous, unmarked mounds. The plan is a most creditable effort and I have often wondered why more churches do not have something of the sort on display. If successful, Thomas Hardy's churchyard lament will be happily repudiated at Bilsington –

'Where we are huddled none can trace,
And if our names remain,
They pave some path, or porch or place
Where we have never lain.'

Perched on the edge of the escarpment that encircles the landward side of Romney Marsh, St. Matthew's is one of a string of churches (Bonnington, Bilsington and Kenardington are the others) that lie a mile or so back from the road that runs from Hythe to Tenterden. An escape from today's traffic, but an arrangement which suggests that an older road once linked the four, though there was no sign of one on the ground or on my map. As with the other churches, the Royal Military Canal runs below, but here it is crossed by the railway from Rye to Ashford. In the short two hours that my wife and I were there, three trains went by. I cannot imagine that there is much demand for its services, but it must be one of the more pleasant stretches of line in the county, if not the country.

One can hardly describe Warehorne and ignore the tower. This is a mainly Decorated church and apparently the original tower was partly destroyed by lightning in 1777. Its replacement is of brick and of the plainest, bleakest design that I have seen. Writing in 1922, Charles Igglesden condemned it as being in the 'worst possible taste' and lamented that the climbing ivy did not cover more of its severe and featureless facade. He would have been more disappointed today for what ivy there was has been stripped away and the only vegetation to soften the outline is a clump or two of greenery that has established a foothold on the inaccessible parapet string course. Considering the rest of the church and its setting, the tower must rank as an architectural snub to the medieval past and a conceit for the dictates of its own time.

My view of the church avoids this tower and concentrates on the windows, despite the fact that they are much more difficult to draw. The two facing differ from the others. Unlike the rest, the east window of the chancel is Perpendicular and very fine it looks. The east window to the north aisle is a peculiarity; Pevsner says it 'must have been tampered with'. I think it was originally square headed, but that when they restored one on the south side, the discarded arch was added as a sort of fanlight to give that round-headed effect; I could, of course, very easily be mistaken. There is a south doorway and a north porch. The doorway is unused and boarded but obviously old to judge by the scratch dials on the jamb. The north porch is contemporary with the tower, red brick but improved by a 'compass gable' – something that gives it a surprisingly Dutch appearance. The door was locked, but bore an undated notice saying 'the church will be closed today' – rather a subtle way of effecting a twenty-four hour closure for as long as the author chooses.

One could see the interior relatively clearly and quite visible were the box pews and the elegant marble columns of the arcades. The chancel was empty of stalls and a communion table had been placed below the chancel arch. Seen from the outside, the result was light and airy, but with a somewhat puritan flavour – perhaps the attitudes that produced the uncompromising tower in the 18th century still persist in the management of the interior today.

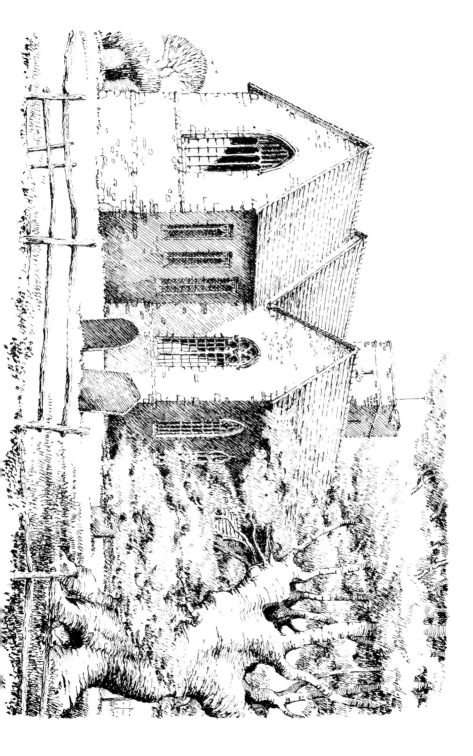

ADDINGTON   *Eadda's farmstead*
St. Margaret

Although its tower is visible from afar, the church itself is hidden behind its dense screen of yews and chestnut trees. It can be found on its hillock, comfortably withdrawn from the local roads, but well within earshot of the M20 in the valley below. One might have expected this prime site to have been pre-empted by the ancient Britons who built their megalithic burial chamber under a mile away in a far less favoured position. These prehistoric stones, like the church, are not easy to find and indeed the ladies whom I consulted in the village shop were none too specific in their directions. It is curious that within a span of six miles in this part of Kent there should be four separate prehistoric sites − a primitive Piccadilly Circus almost.

To come to the church: it is originally early Norman with a robust Perpendicular west tower, but there has been much rearrangement as I hope my sketch will show. It was locked when I drew it, but I had previously seen the inside when the Friends of Kent Churches descended. I admit I should have retained a lasting impression of its contents, but I can remember little − there are some exceptional brasses and a south chapel largely devoted to the memorials of one family. In a church of such age there are bound to be several features of great interest and one can only feel inadequate at one's failure to do them justice.

In deciding which view to attempt I had a choice of the churchyard path leading uphill, past rows of venerable tombstones, to the mellow north porch, or of the east front dominated by that grey stone obelisk. Despite the attraction of the porch's carved oak bargeboard (not easy to draw) the 18th century obelisk won. From this direction one can clearly make out the outline of the window in the south chapel which the Wattons blocked in order to hang their monumental memorial inside. Who can blame them? The memorial is very distinguished, undoubtedly more remarkable than the window it displaces, but as a purist, one would have preferred the blocking of the Victorian window of the north chapel. Unfortunately they were two hundred years too early. One can also discern traces of some rearrangement, or re-windowing, in the east front of the chancel, but here courses of herring-bone masonry survive to confirm the early dating. The whole effect of this end of the church, watched by that monolithic obelisk − itself not too dissimilar from those unimaginably ancient megaliths − is intriguing and demonstrates that meddling with the original is not always disastrous.

The last thing that I noticed before packing up to depart in search of the prehistoric stones was a nearby tree − a 'royal oak' from Windsor Great Park, planted in June 1953 to commemorate the coronation of Elizabeth II. In the thirty-two years that this oak has been growing at Addington it has achieved a height of some thirty feet and a trunk diameter of roughly one foot. I wonder if that is a normal rate of growth or whether the oak has obtained some arboreal benefit from its position in consecrated ground. One would hope so and a long life to boot.

SHADOXHURST
St. Peter and St. Paul

. . . ? wooded hill

Shadoxhurst can hardly be called a village – more an extended rural locality with cottages and bungalows at intervals lining the lanes which here converge. There is virtually no sign of any past concentration of country folk so why the surprising little church just five miles south west of Ashford, less now that Ashford has expanded so much. Could it have been an episcopal excuse for raising tithes – what an unworthy thought. More likely a penance for past indiscretions.

Here, however, the little old church has been – for a very long time with the first recorded vicar appointed in 1289. That dating puts the fabric at the start of the Decorated period whereas Pevsner claims Early English for the chancel – no doubt rightly because the church would have to be built before the first incumbent could be appointed. It consists briefly of a diminutive nave and chancel which are saved from the commonplace by the bellcote perched uneasily on the western buttresses. This church is well worth coming to see for such a curious arrangement alone and the only thing remotely similar that I can remember is the small turret at Acrise, that secluded and secretive little downland church. My sketch makes the most of this singular feature, which one could not possibly overlook, but I was sorely tempted to substitute some nice old weathered tombstones for those 19th century squared-off specimens you see between the churchyard pines. Honesty won – it is chancing your arm to be dishonest in a churchyard.

Inside one becomes even more conscious of the atmosphere of miniaturisation. I did not count the number of pews, obtained in 1977 from a redundant church, but there were not many of them. In the case of Admiral Molloy's marble memorial in the chancel, on the other hand, there is no false modesty. His achievements in life – sixty years in the navy, the ships he commanded, participation in the battle of Malaga, when the French Mediterranean fleet attempted to recapture Gibraltar – all are faithfully recorded in a detailed inscription below his sad-looking bust surrounded by nautical impedimenta. Like the bellcote, the admiral is also well worth coming to see. There is no tower to the church, but a clock nevertheless; its workings are here installed in a glass case in the nave for all to see and for all to hear as well, as the weighty pendulum swings rhythmically backwards and forwards below.

To complete the idiosyncratic features of Shadoxhurst one must include the 'church school' close by the churchyard gate. This little extravaganza, folly almost, built in 1846 is more an elaboration of gables and dormer windows than anything else; an attempt it would seem to enclose the minimum space within the maximum display of ornamental stonework. The 'school' appeared to be deserted and deteriorating but there were signs, as far as one could tell, that restoration or decoration might be in progress or in contemplation. I hope so – an original little church is made even more singular with such a guardian at the gate.

ORLESTONE
St. Mary the Virgin

Ordlaf's farmstead

As a description, 'five miles from anywhere' would fit Orlestone church to a T. It lies in the wooded hinterland behind Romney Marsh with no village that I could find. Down a lane off the main road, more of a drive really with young trees planted and staked at intervals, one comes on a terminal group of manor house, farm and church. Of the three, I suppose the manor house looks best. It all seemed very isolated and solitary when I was there, a consequence of the first industrial revolution which emptied the countryside in favour of the town, and the second big change which replaced the remaining farm workers by the more economic machines. A hundred years ago there would have been labourers and their families about, I am sure; today nothing but a police car that came past to visit the farm – about a lost sheep, no doubt. There cannot be much in the way of crime here, or even of sin, with no-one left to commit it.

The church, although dating from the 14th century, has a Victorian air externally which stems from the thorough restoration of 1883. The repaired walls look as if they were built yesterday with no trace of dilapidation to soften the uniformity or to erode the pointing. What a pity that the best of intentions should be so rewarded but still, if the Victorians have extended the life of this church by an extra five hundred years, who should criticise. Like Shadoxhurst, which it somewhat resembles, the church consists of a nave and chancel, but here the porch is attached to the medieval doorway at the western end. Above this porch, and below the shingled bellcote, is an odd looking window. Applying my amateur architectural deductive skill I concluded that it had been a conventional Decorated window of which the lower two thirds has been removed for some reason. My deductions were confirmed and my self-esteem gratified, as I sat considering this in the porch, by spotting under the benches supporting fragments of antique stone moulding – lo and behold, the tracery that once might have formed the cusped arches of the displaced mullions from the semi-blocked window. I wonder if I was right – it seems unlikely that bench seats should need intricately carved stonework underneath.

The churchyard, as befits a lonely, locked church, was immaculate; grass recently cut, fences and gate in repair and so on; but possibly a shade over-treed – definitely so from the direction of the lane. Instead of yews the churchyard grew those elegant, branchy pines, a species I have never managed to identify, which are almost as good as yews and more fun to draw. As I pondered how to attempt the church, simplicity itself compared to some, I realised for the umpteenth time that the less church there is the more compensating surroundings there will necessarily be and the greater the difficulty. Orlestone demonstrates this precisely – very little church in my sketch, much foliage in its place. That sounds as if the sketch is a fabrication; not so, the church is hidden and unobserved by all except the persistent.

All Saints

This church, on the hillside above the Medway opposite Teston church, has long reproached me for neglect. What one can see, as one drives along the crowded road to Maidstone, are orderly ranks of soft fruit vegetation rising from the river, a farm with oasts, clusters of tall trees and, in the midst of all, the grey stone tower of the church. It looks perfect – a Rowland Hilder picture – and yet it has taken fourteen years of living nearby to come and do it, faithfully, if not excitingly.

Why the delay? Well, close to one is at first discouraged. The farm and the fields around remain as typically Kent as ever, but the church falls from grace because, except for the tower which is as recent as 1523, the original walls have been comprehensively smothered in stucco. The nave and chancel were built in about 1100 thus making it a complete Norman survival. Perhaps the hidden ragstone walls have crumbled more than is usual with other churches of a comparable age – hence the drastic cure. To someone like myself, who has no responsibility for maintenance, the cure here seems worse than the disease; nevertheless the medicine was applied but with an apologetic spirit, I think, for at the eastern corners of the chancel the overlay has been carefully trimmed back to reveal the pitted quoin stones of tufa beneath. As it is so old there are unfortunately no helpful buttresses, not even at the tower, to break the line and produce a relieving shadow. And that is what has discouraged me.

The churchyard is a pleasure to wander in. Well stocked with elegant tombstones and evenly distributed with mature English yews, there are, as a bonus, one or two of those grey-blue cedars which always add a touch of the exotic to an otherwise conventional scene. The churchyard path is lined with young, golden topiary yews and these, given time, will surely rival those at Brenchley. Nothing here in any way disconcerts the eye.

The church was locked but displayed the usual notice as to where the key might be found – in my experience often miles away or protected by loose and ill-disposed dogs. Imagine my delight, then, to find on packing up that the door had mysteriously become unlocked. Once in the tiny nave, the memory of all that rendering outside is rapidly dispelled by the sight of the great round Norman arch to the chancel. Just think of the satisfaction of building an arch in stone and saying to oneself – 'There. God willing, that will still be standing in eight hundred years' time'. To accompany this majestic arch there is an appropriate gallery of sculpted memorial tablets on the surrounding walls, of which the most prominent is a hanging monument to a local worthy, his wife, six sons and five daughters. When Arthur Mee saw this memorial, the father was missing from the family group. When I saw it, he was there all right but minus his head. How odd! Even for 1605, their epitaph below is cheerfully erratic, the spelling of the surname and repeated words changing within the course of only a few lines. One wonders how the eleven children divided their patrimony and whether they continued to enjoy this church and live in the countryside around West Farleigh. It cannot have changed very much since their day.

WEST STOURMOUTH
All Saints

This little church lies at the end of the road that points towards the junction of the Great and Little Stour rivers where once they discharged into the sea when Thanet really was an island. In terms of agriculture the church is in the fields, in terms of the 20th century it is nowhere and in terms of the Church, it is redundant. That much I expected. What I had not hoped for was to find it open.

Its external appearance is quite enough to attract any fancier of old churches. The churchyard is more packed with gravestones than most and my sketch depicts, in the foreground, a regimented row of head, foot and body stones, one of several. There could have been many more people here in the 18th and 19th centuries than there are today. It does not in fact need very many; one hundred and fifty at a service and the church would be crowded. The walls are a delightful mixture of flints, tufa, rubble and cobble stones, bricks, Roman tiles and cement; all combined haphazardly in complete harmony if not stability. Lack of stability has called forth reinforcement by enormous brick buttresses at the western end under the wooden turret and on the north side of the chancel where the walls tend uneasily outwards. Furthermore, in pursuit of structural integrity, the wall of the north aisle has been lowered, windows blocked, the roof carried down and dormer windows inserted to give an oddly domestic look to this side of the church.

Although now in the care of the Redundant Churches Fund, it was not yet open to the public, but I was lucky enough for my visit to coincide with work in progress. Two young men were within; they admitted me and could not have been more helpful in discussing this or that particular. They had so far attended to the roof timbers, limewashed or plastered the walls, treated the dark carved furniture for woodworm and were now in process of giving the box pews and stalls a dressing of heated beeswax as a preservative. Even if no longer fulfilling its religious function, the church as a result looks cared for and, rather like the navy's ships laid up in reserve, well able to resist deterioration and ready for reactivation if necessary. The most obvious features are the arcade pillars, the good tiled floor with its ledger stones and the 1475 brass, and the uncovered altar stone which exhibited a rough simplicity and strength that normally lies concealed under the altar cloth. Revealed are its five consecration crosses; the arcade pillars bear similar, if less precise, marks but these we concluded were 'thanksgiving' crosses for a safe return from the wars – rather as with our 'crusader' crosses at Hadlow.

All Saints is a very old church with a blocked Saxon window to prove it. Let us say it is one thousand years old in parts. With those massive buttresses to prevent any further slippage and its good sound roof, preservation and protection by the Redundant Churches Fund should, barring accidents, make it good for another thousand years which, no doubt, is what the Fund intends.

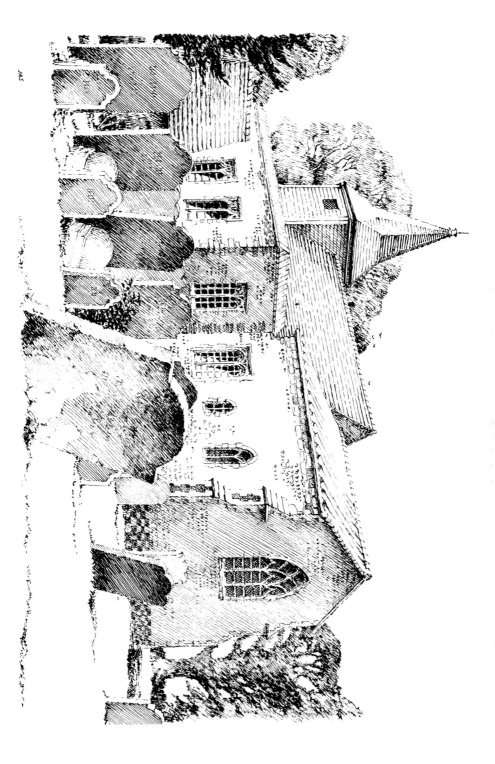

JAS

PRESTON
St. Mildred

Priest's farmstead

This Early English church lies at the head of a lane well away from its village, sufficiently far to need a helpful lady's directions. There is a farm, a pair of white-washed cottages, where the key is kept, and, opposite, Preston Court. It was on the site of Preston Court that the Infanta of Kent, otherwise known as the Countess of Huntington, had her palace in the 14th century, the remains of which are said to lie below the surface of one of the Court's large ponds. No sign of medieval masonry there now – only skimming swallows and martins. It is not clear from the church's pamphlet why this church is dedicated to St. Mildred, who, although abbess of the convent at Minster, never appears to have visited Preston. The Infanta, who died here in 1367, would seem to have a better claim, particularly as the present structure relates more to her date than it does to Mildred's.

Externally the church is remarkable for the four conspicuous dormer windows that act as a sort of clerestory on the sloping roofs. They compensate for the small Early English windows of the aisles which are now blocked. Very decorative the latter look for red bricks, bleached by the sun, have been used to fill the interstices of the stone tracery and thus produce a pleasant patterned effect – well worth the loss of light inside. The church consists of an unbuttressed west tower, nave and chancel, north and south aisles and north chapel and is really quite substantial for a village of the size of Preston. The chapel, which apparently was used as a Victorian village school, has a small corner-fireplace – to warm the children, no doubt, after a longish walk in the winter. It has all the flavour of that enchanting book of country childhood, 'Lark Rise to Candleford'. An aspect of the nave and aisles which is unusual, both visually and architecturally, is the differing heights of the separating arches, those to the south being loftier than those on the north side. As such, they do seem to be rather in the same category as a bridge which, built from either river bank, fails to meet in the middle. However the arches date from the 14th century so stability cannot be a problem.

Before finding the church I had a sandwich lunch at the village pub, the 'Half Moon and Seven Stars' which, like any parish church, proudly exhibits an unbroken sequence of licensees from 1676. This pub is home for local teams of 'bat and trap' cricket – much played in this part of Kent, I was told. The game seems to be some-thing of a cross between skittles and French cricket and I am sure leads to many convivial and profitable evenings. Being the solitary lunch-time customer, I was shown the carefully mown pitch in the garden, the hard composition ball and other esoteric technicalities so altogether my lunchtime at the Half Moon was not unlike exploring a church for the first time – full of surprises and unexpected pleasures.

MONKTON
St. Mary Magdalene

Monks' farmstead

Monkton must be the most unprotected church in Kent, much like Reculver in exposure. It stands on that level plain between the mainland and Thanet which has been rescued from the sea since the Romans landed a few miles away at Richborough. There is no shelter from the wind and little insulation from the rigours of continental winters. There are brave trees around the expansive churchyard, it is true, but no yews. Whether that is due to the elements or something to do with sheep (the monks had two thousand here when they farmed the manor) it is difficult to say. At all events it must be the weather that has left its imprint so indelibly on the fabric. I have never seen a church so eroded; between the cobblestones and flints the mortar is excavated to a depth of two or three inches in places. It is astonishing that they hold together – but they have done, ever since 1190 in fact.

All this is very apparent as one faces that splendidly simple and primitive tower. No buttresses, no elaborate windows, no embattled parapet – just an old weather-beaten door at the foot and a few unaffected Early English lancets, blocked in some cases. It has an aura of antiquity that one can almost touch. In the 15th century the tower received its third stage but the nave suffered more drastic attention. One can see fairly clearly on the north side the outline of five arches which once constituted the arcade to a vanished north aisle. I imagine that the withdrawal of the monks to Canterbury occasioned that retrenchment. The south windows are Perpendicular and, although relatively recent, have succumbed more obviously to the effects of the weather, the mullions of one in particular being so worn that a gap now exists between glass and stone. Perhaps it was always the practice of medieval masons to use a softer sandstone when they came to apply their chisels – that could account for the elaborate moulding and for the existence of much Victorian replacement everywhere.

Inside, the accommodation is spare and economic to a degree – a straightforward narrow nave and chancel enclosed by walls on which the old plaster has developed a lovely soft, mottled, complexion. It is on a par, artistically and chronologically speaking, with the broken surface of the tower. One wonders how either escaped the restoration of 1860, but perhaps they were too busy raising the chancel floor and cutting back the rising level of the churchyard outside. Let us hope it continues inviolate and in this age of respect for the past I should imagine that it will.

It is bound to be cold in here in winter but, thoughtfully, warm blue curtains are provided to screen the front few pews from draughts and one can appreciate how wise they were to eliminate the north aisle in anticipation of a reduced lay congregation with less fortitude than that of the ascetic brethren. The monks have retreated; the parishioners are fewer and less religious and the grander St. Nicholas-at-Wade is well within visibility distance; three pointers towards redundancy for Monkton, although the enthusiasm of the young couple I met there promises resistance to any such fate.

140

JAS

ST. NICHOLAS AT WADE
St. Nicholas

Ford or wading place

Described by Pevsner as 'one of the most rewarding churches in the north east corner of the county', St. Nicholas' is certainly grand. Why so grand is not clear to me for the village is little more than a hamlet even if it once controlled a crossing of the River Wansum – now an inconspicuous dyke in the fields. I imagine that the monks at Canterbury, with their manors spread about this fertile tract, may have had a hand in its inception. One can visualise the abbot consulting with his chapter as to how best to acknowledge the abbey's satisfaction with the fruits of its granaries and what better way than to build a church of thanksgiving. If this is how their minds worked, they spared no expense to give effect to their thoughts, at all stages of its construction, to their, or somebody else's, lasting credit and our benefit. The result is worthy of their receipts. For instance, the clerestoried nave and aisles are embattled, as are the imposing tower and porch, the buttresses are diapered with flint, the tower is walled with close-set knapped flints and the porch is storied – all signs in a remote country church of 'conspicuous consumption' if not extravagance. Generous benefactions continue: the excellent limestone statue of St. Nicholas in the porch is a modern example.

The inside is a match for the exterior, the arches lining the nave receiving twenty-one lines of Pevsner's scholarship in his description of the church. My impression of these arches is that there appeared to be none to support the tower at the western end of the south aisle. Perhaps it was the ledger stones which distracted me from the foundations of the tower. These memorials stretch, without interruption, from one side of the church to the other and then up the gangway between the nave and north aisle to end in the north chapel on top of a chest-tomb. The ecclesiastical equivalents of domestic Persian rugs, ledger stones are by far the best paving for any church floor and, as here, for the lid of a family monument; a family which incidentally includes a poet laureate amongst its number. This distinction makes St. Nicholas the second church in Kent that I have sketched which is associated with a poet laureate – the other being Boxley with Tennyson.

The single example of economy in this church is the surprisingly crude rustic ladder, not staircase, to the chamber above the porch. The door at the perilous summit of this contrivance was locked, but I could see that the room is used for storage; once it was the local plumber's workshop. Both usages seem derogatory, not to say sacrilegious, and out of character with the rest of the church. Assuming it is large enough, my solution would be to use the chamber as a depository or library for records of particular interest to the church and village. A long-life diary might be kept to note great events, say a Visitation by the Queen or merely the passing of yet another peaceful year, entered with formal ceremony by the parish clerk and toasted with a glass of wine annually. 'Keep the ladder' would be my only stipulation; its primitive unsophistication serves to emphasise the splendid proportions of the rest of the church.

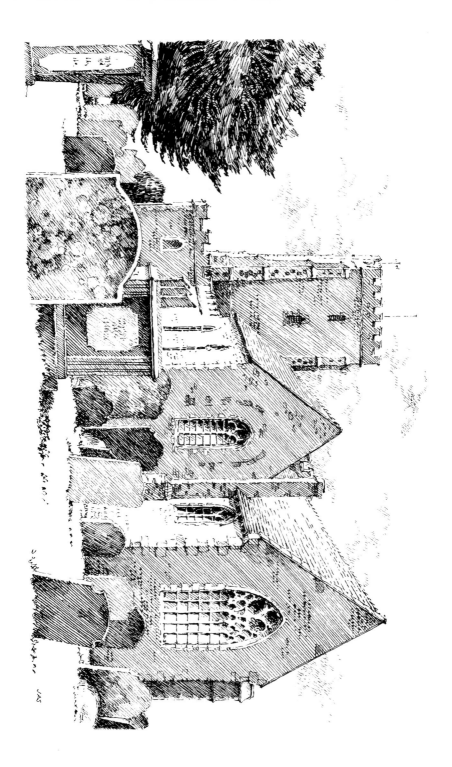

Looking at this church today one would never imagine what a drama took place here in the Middle Ages. To be exact, the drama took place half a mile away at the preceptory of the Knights Hospitallers of St. John when King John, under threat of invasion by the French, agreed with the papal legate to acknowledge the Pope as his overlord and to pay an annual tribute in exchange for the lifting of the decree of excommunication on king and people. The cause of the interdict was disagreement over the appointment of the Archbishop of Canterbury but, if one analyses the rapprochement rationally, it would seem that the Pope was selling salvation and the king buying it – strictly commercial and political in reality. The preceptory still stands. For long years it was used as a farmhouse, now it is an anaesthetised national monument in the absentee care of the Department of the Environment – rather sad and lonely in its fenced-off enclosure.

The church, though, bears no trace of that inglorious day in May 1213; in fact not too much of it can have been standing then, just the nave probably and part of the chancel. As one approaches, it is the 15th century tower with its semi-circular stair turret which most obviously distinguishes Swingfield from the generality of Kent's churches. One might almost be looking at a church in Norfolk. There is much brickwork in the tower's buttresses which suggests repairs fairly recently, possibly when the north aisle was added in 1870 – why on earth did they do that, I wonder. One enters the church through an endearing little wooden porch of the 14th century, in which incidentally the barrow for biers is stored, and proceeds under an older, smaller doorway bearing the markings of two scratch dials. Inside, simplicity is the keystone and certainly there is no evidence of the erstwhile presence of the Knights Hospitallers. On the face of it, nothing but peace and innocence can have reigned in the parish and Pope Innocent's anathemas have vanished with the wind. More ominous seems the moralising inscription on a ledger stone of 1677 –

> 'Death fears no colours, drums, guns, pike or blade
> All these give place unto the fatall Spade'

The church was locked, but the key was not far away. To obtain it from a bungalow called 'Goldilocks', I had to pass 'Wye Wurrie', 'Dollar Gap' and 'Little Siberia' – as fanciful a crop of names as I have ever met. The pub facing the church, where I had lunch, was more conventionally named the Three Bells – inaccurately now as two of the church's three bells were sold to pay for repairs to the roof. It is a pleasant little country pub, but the publican is trying to sell it. In many ways its future resembles that of a country church. Leave it unmodernised and nobody comes; modernise to attract the custom, or the congregation, and the magic departs. The preceptory has been put in deep freeze; the pub may close but at least the un-modernised church functions and can still be opened. Let us hope it may remain so.

JAS

ELHAM
St. Mary

Eel meadow

With Elham church enjoying the unanimous approval of the discriminating, it is difficult to explain why I found it a disappointment or, to put it the other way round and to apply the criticism to myself rather than to the church, why I failed to appreciate its quality. Dug firmly into a steep eastward slope, it lies in the heart of its village above the Nailbourne stream. Immediately to the north of the church-yard there is a particularly picturesque enclosed square which is rather reminiscent of Chilham and, similarly, must tend to turn Elham village and church into a magnet for the idle sightseer out for a day in the country. Swingfield, from whence I had just come, will never become a tourist trap and perhaps the contrast is why my admiration for Elham was somewhat qualified.

The church itself is more noted for its rich interior than for the outside, although the latter is not without its distinction and eccentricities; for instance the almost detached gabled north porch through which one enters. Conspicuous above the grey walls of the main structure is the tall, ribbed spire; it looks to be an afterthought to a perfectly good Perpendicular tower and indeed a photograph in the church pamphlet of a May Day scene conveys an impression of a spireless tower. This cannot be correct; the spire must antedate photography and I suppose the omission should be attributed to a trick of the light. The pamphlet includes one of those helpful hatched plans which provide a key to the dates of the various parts of the fabric. Here the building campaigns run from the 12th century arcade piers, the oldest part, to the modern buttresses at the corners of the chancel. The south side is 13th century, the north 14th and the porch and tower, 15th — a very orderly progression.

So to the ornately decorated and celebrated interior which, I feel, might be taken for a Catholic church on the Continent; only the absence of statues betrays the Reformation. It is the woodwork that must first arouse the admiration of anyone who has ever nailed two pieces of wood together or applied a coat of varnish. Sixty years ago there must have been master craftsmen here at Elham for they made in the village the beautifully finished pews — walnut inlaid with rosewood — and their predecessor, the unusually grand churchwardens' pew at the foot of the tower. All around, the walls are panelled and nowhere on all this polished woodwork was there the slightest suspicion of dust. They had medieval craftsmen here too and their handiwork is perpetuated in the collection chest, a hollow trunk of yew, polished and shining now, but with its original contours still preserved. It is a match, in its primitive strength, for the worn stone coffin lid that lies inconspicuously on the floor in a corner.

The Continental impression comes from the gilded reredos behind the altar, from the icon above the ancient pillar shrine and from what Pevsner describes as a 'Florentine quattrocento' tabernacle above the font. There are framed oil paintings and traces of a wall painting, grotesque corbel heads and a 'faldstool' carved with the arms of Bourbon and Medici. All of which goes to show how obtuse one must be if one fails to enjoy such a treasure house.

UPPER HARDRES
St. Peter and St. Paul

Hard, stony ground

Hard, stony ground though it may have seemed when first the name became current, this tract of the North Downs astride the Roman road below Canterbury looked to me in late August to be a farmer's or landowner's paradise. And thus it must have been for the Hardres family when they came over with the Conqueror. They perforce brought this church here for there is nothing much else at Upper Hardres other than their Court and a few estate houses and cottages. There is a monstrous great barn by the old gatehouse, no doubt necessarily gigantic to accommodate the bountiful crops — so the farming and harvesting continues. But not the Norman family which once acted as host to Henry VIII and was rewarded with his hunting knife for its pains — which could have been considerable; I would be surprised if Henry ever travelled with an economical retinue. The family has been replaced by a nursing home, but not before there were the will and the resources to build this flint church. How fortunate we are that self-interested landowners should bequeath such imperishable relics for the common weal today for without their presence I doubt if the Deanery of West Bridge would have sanctioned a church here — on the stony ground.

The church is of that curious plan in which the tower interrupts the run of the south aisle; presumably the tower, being Norman, was there first and the aisle was built around it — it makes a change from the almost universal west tower which always seems to me to be the wrong end for the most prominent external feature of a church. It is the porch, however, which I found most attractive — a long, low, covered approach to the Tudor(?) doorway. Its ceiling is boarded in trefoil section and the jambs are constructed from round stone pillars, taken from elsewhere, I am sure.

The church was locked and the key over a mile away in the next village, but a new glass door has been installed in the west end of the nave and one can obtain a clear, if restricted, view of the interior. This glass door, protected by wrought iron-work, is a distinct asset and must be a form of memorial. As is to be expected, the church is rich in memorials, in stained glass, and is the possessor of a celebrated brass — none of which, of course, I could see. What I could see were chairs instead of pews, a Norman font crowned with a most elegant Georgian cover, a handsome chandelier of the same period — enough to make me regret the absent key.

In the porch was a notice beginning 'X, by Divine Permission Lord Bishop of Dover'. 'By Divine Providence', I have since learnt is reserved for the two arch-bishops and the Bishop of Durham — all others are 'by permission'! This phrase, obviously hallowed by tradition, reads to the uncommitted like a heavenly prime minister dispensing ministerial appointments. The announcement declares that the benefices of Upper Hardres and Stelling are to remain unfilled for the next five years, but that there is to be a priest-in-charge who is shortly to be installed by the rural dean; all is therefore not lost here and, if the present state of the church and churchyard is anything to go by, the priest will have little to worry about and reliable allies in discharging his responsibilities in this corner of Kent.

NACKINGTON
St. Mary the Virgin

With Canterbury less than five miles to the north, one would not expect to find a church of quite such rural unsophistication so close to the seat of ecclesiastical pomp and power as one does at Nackington. Although completely enclosed by three farms and their fields, it could not possibly be considered remote and yet it displays all the external characteristics of some hamlet church lost in a fold of the Downs — for instance diminutive size, no lychgate and only a simple grassy path through rather an empty churchyard.

The nave is Norman, the chancel and chapel 13th century with Victorian additions in the shape of a vestry on the south side and a porch on the north. The tower, though, is the eccentricity here; I have never seen one like it before. To start with, it is not even symmetrical with the western gable; then the 13th century stone stage barely reaches above the eaves of the nave. Above the stone first stage is Victorian brickwork topped self-consciously by ridiculous brick battlements which never manage to reach the ridge of the roof. Notwithstanding a miniature spire, any construction that fails to dominate can hardly be called a tower, but that is obviously what it originally set out to be. What happened to its 13th century upper stages, if they ever existed, one can only conjecture; the Victorians were uncharacteristically restrained here in their work, but then they had only to provide for one bell so perhaps that was their excuse for so meagre a completion or restoration. At any rate, as a result of the evident economy, there is nothing quite like Nackington church in my experience and that makes it an unexpected pleasure to find and sketch.

On entering through the Victorian porch, one is greeted by an extract from the report after an archdeacon's visitation in the mid 1550s which reads — 'They present that the chauncel ther (sic) is sore in ruyne and decay, that the priest cannot stand drye'. No danger of that today; as I sketched two men were repairing the lead flashing in the valley between chapel and chancel. The interior too has received more than usual loving care and attention in the past, witness the screen and linenfold around the walls of nave and chapel — carved and subscribed for by ten parishioners whose names are carefully inscribed in a section of the panelling. Less successful was the misguided installation of central heating which now looks old-fashioned and cumbersome and obscures the better flags beneath. Nevertheless not without its own pretensions to grandeur, Nackington church possesses a pulpit which is decorated with coats of arms — to impress a congregation, I calculate, for whom there is seating for no more than seventy-five.

The church, say Pevsner and the pamphlet, is notable for its stained glass which dates from the 13th century and some of which, it is rumoured, came from Canterbury cathedral. At least if proximity to a cathedral city diminishes a country church, there are compensations when works of art, no longer needed by the great, descend to decorate the humble.

Unless they have special reasons, I doubt if many people visit Stowting church nowadays. It is not famous for its architecture, no celebrities are associated with it, so far as I know, and it is not easy to find. It lies inconspicuously in an embrace of the Downs roughly half way between Ashford and Dover. I drove through the hamlet twice before I located the church hiding a mile away with the village school. Even then I had a job to find the entrance path so one might expect to find here an 'unimproved' medieval church. But the Victorians found it all right and restored the 13th century fabric to such an extent that one might almost be looking at a 19th century building. Maintenance continues; as I sketched, the vicar and two parishioners discussed the state of the roof and carefully identified the odd missing or fractured tile. If my roof at home was half as good as Stowting's, I should have less to worry about.

The church consists of nave, chancel and north aisle plus a north west tower and an equally tall chimney stack. The chief impression one receives on entering is one of gloom due, I think, to the lofty ceilings and inadequate lighting from the windows. Of the furniture, the most evocative pieces are the old choir stalls with their carved poppy-head bench ends. The literature and items on display reflect the village school by the gate – children's drawings, pamphlets etc. with an emphasis on aiding the 'third world' and on problems of race. As such, they seemed to me to reflect sociology more than religion but, no doubt, I am not in tune with modern pastoral thinking. It is a widespread development and one sees it in practically every church.

Undertaken in the long wet grass of September and with nettles threatening the nape of my neck, my view of the church shows quite a substantial building of unknapped, coursed flints, no sign of the original walling since the chancel was so largely reconstructed in the 1840s and the north aisle and tower were added ten years later. One cannot say it is a modest building and the statistics for Stowting scarcely justify its dimensions – in 1984 there was an adult population of one hundred and sixty-five, an electoral roll of thirty and an average attendance at the parish communion of just under twenty. The surprising figure (to me) is that of attendance at Christmas and Easter when the average Sunday congregation no more than doubled. Stowting does, though, seem to fare better than its three co-parishes under the same priest-in-charge.

Reading through the above remarks, I seem to detect a somewhat disparaging tone which is really quite unfair to a church and its parishioners who in a previous generation took more trouble than most to preserve what they had. There is more a case here at Stowting for congratulations than for criticism.

ELMSTED
St. James the Great

Elm homestead

No one could possibly pass Elmsted church and not give it a second glance. It is the top-heavy tower which is such a stopper here: Early English stonework, supported by a massive Elizabethan brick buttress and crowned by an overlapping wooden belfry and spire — this unbalanced construction makes an unforgettable finial to an isolated summit on the Downs. Alone in its churchyard, with but a farm and farmhouse for company, no village, I cannot imagine why the church is here at all, but how splendid that it should be.

Striking and bizarre as the tower may be, it in no way upstages the interior, rather the reverse in fact. To start with, the church was unlocked, remarkable enough considering the lonely situation (the only animated life I saw was a truculent Jack Russell). To return to the interior, it is light and airy, made more so by the removal of all pews except those in the nave. Bare of clutter the arcade pillars, which are 15th century, are revealed as standing on the square bases of their Norman predecessors — one would never see that so clearly with the aisle pews in place. Here and there, where the arches spring from the walls, carved corbel heads look down, one of which as always, puts out its tongue. I do not know what significance there is in this habit, but it cannot have been simply a rude gesture on the part of the mason; the church authorities would never have allowed that so possibly it is some sort of defiance of the devil. In the pewless north and south chapels one can appreciate to the full the virtual monopoly of memorials enjoyed by the Honeywood family. They carpet the floor and decorate the walls. One male member is recorded as being 'Controwler of ye Revenue of Tenthes and First Fruits'. It sounds a sinecure and a good thing to be. The south, Honeywood, chapel possesses an altar stone, recovered from the churchyard; I had always understood that altar stones bear inscribed 'consecration' crosses but this monolith bore none that I could find. Who am I, though, to doubt the church pamphlet? Of equal interest are the bolster marks on the stonework of the north and south doors. Here I read that the oblique strokes are the marks of Norman masons, the neater, vertical claw marks those of later medieval working. One cannot avoid a warm feeling of closeness to the past as one contemplates those eight hundred year old scratches or resist running one's fingers over the beaten surface of the dressed stones.

Before leaving, I counted the headstones that have been cleared from the churchyard grass to line the perimeter fence; there are sixty-seven of them. They were moved to facilitate mowing and keeping down the weeds and brambles. From that point of view, clearance is obviously a sensible move; from an aesthetic point of view, it is misguided in my opinion; from an ethical point of view, it seems dubious and not something I would care to authorise. Elmsted is striking enough anyway and can well stand such desecration, but many churches where this 'efficiency' policy is adopted are made to look sadly deserted and deprived.

BROOMFIELD
St. Margaret

Open land where broom grows

Despite five halcyon years exploring and sketching Kent's country churches, it was only when I read a local newspaper article about Broomfield that I became aware of its existence at all. The article commemorated an event that took place one Sunday morning forty five years ago, on my birthday anniversary to be exact, when a German Dornier bomber crashed in the strawberry field above the church. Fortunately the church suffered no damage but two members of the crew were temporarily buried in the churchyard. No strawberry field, no scar of the crash nor headstone to the casualties now remain to mark the approach of war to the placid fields of Broomfield – it is an aggression worth remembering though.

This is a deceptive little church, plain as can be externally with no frills and within a churchyard on the slope of a hill that almost puts one in mind of Devon. There is no village, simply a scattered farming community, but what is significant, if invisible, is the presence of Leeds castle less than a mile away. The lords of the castle would seem to have made no effort to enlarge or enrich the church but they did patronise it to the extent of internment beneath the nave – a surprising choice when one remembers that the much more distinguished church of St. Nicholas at Leeds village is equidistant from the castle. The small nave is Norman, with blocked windows to prove it, and the squat tower Perpendicular – but only just sufficiently perpendicular to overlook the ridge of the nave roof. The chancel, though, is newer, having been rebuilt in 1749 by the lady owner of the house in Leeds village which replaced the 12th century priory there; why did she bother about next-door Broomfield? Perhaps the vicar was a friend and persuasive.

The church was locked, of course, and the grass in the churchyard long enough and wet enough to conjure the fields of pasture which surround its hawthorn hedge. As the building is small, the window ledges being to scale were accessible so that one might have inspected the interior but for the stained glass. I do not know whether it is standard practice, but here at Broomfield there is a narrow, one inch-wide margin of clear glass around the coloured opaque panels and this transparent ribbon permits a surprisingly generous view beyond. There were no monuments on the walls so far as I could see and I was, of course, denied any sight of the resting place of the Lord Fairfax of Leeds Castle who, Arthur Mee says, had the misfortune to die when his family fortunes had ebbed to non-existence in Kent, if not in Virginia. His lordship would find it odd, but not unsatisfactory I dare say, that Leeds Castle now lives in a blaze of publicity while his favoured church languishes unobserved amongst the woods and fields in its lee.

One should never end on a note of criticism but I could not help regretting that anachronistic porch attached to the base of the tower. There is no way in to the church but through the tower; there is though the remnant arch of a nice little ogee window on the north side of the nave which, with imagination, might have been developed into an entrance more in keeping with the rest, I feel. Mr G.M. Hill, who restored the church in 1879, would certainly disagree.

STONE-IN-OXNEY
St. Mary the Virgin

At the stone of . . . in the isle of oxen

Even the confirmed addict of old churches must admit that here at Stone the geological and prehistoric aspects are at least as fascinating as the architecture and atmosphere. The church stands on a bluff overlooking Romney Marsh on the southern extremity of the high ground that once made up the island of Oxney. Four thousand years ago the sea surrounded the island and the tributaries of the River Rother drained directly into the shallow bay that encircled the island; it was not until quite recently, in the 13th century, that the area of the marsh around Oxney was eventually reclaimed to form the landscape that we see today. No doubt it will change again.

Evidence of the fluctuating geological conditions here is now displayed in a glass case behind a 15th century country screen at the base of the tower. Seventy million years ago, dinosaurs roamed the island, if such it then was, and one, an iguanadon, left nine fossilised sections of his tail for us to wonder at. In another age, Lepidotus (a sort of large pike) swam here and left his scales for us to admire. The presence of these fossils in a Christian church whose ministry began only two thousand years ago does tend to confuse the mind a bit.

Besides the monsters (if I am not being too derogatory) in this secluded chamber, there is evidence of a second religion in the shape of a weathered and eroded upright slab of stone, ancient beyond belief (or 1500 years to be roughly proximate), thought to have been dedicated to the Roman cult of Mithras. The dished recess on the top of the altar — for sacrifices? — is still apparent and one can discern quite clearly the worn relief of a bull, passant as they say in heraldry, carved on the vertical face. Once again one's mind is startled — by the juxtaposition of the symbols of the two religions in the same church. The Mithraic stone, in fact, was moved from under the north chapel to a pub, where it was irreverently used as a mounting block, thence to the vicarage garden before returning home to the church. A pagan stone, inscribed with the Mithraic ox and found in an island called Oxney, at a place called Stone, must seem to any romantic mind more than just a coincidence of nomenclature.

A shepherd, who was mustering his sheep with military precision beside the churchyard, volunteered the information that the old wealden priest's house next the church was haunted and that an underground passage connected the two. I do hope he was not pulling the leg of an impressionable visitor.

As to the church, it has that authentic smell of damp that goes with old buildings and grows on one with each encounter. It is now completely Perpendicular in style, having been substantially rebuilt of brownish sandstone after a fire in 1460 destroyed its predecessor. When they did rebuild they seem to have got in a muddle with two small windows in the gable end of the nave; the lower half of each looks down on the chancel, the upper on to the open air. It is a capricious arrangement but entirely in keeping with a Christian church that houses such eccentric relics as a dinosaur's bones and Roman altar. While I was there, a man came in to read the meters. I wonder what the iguanadon would have made of that — eaten him probably.

158

I must admit that Wittersham was a bit of a disappointment and anti-climax coming after Stone-in Oxney and the dinosaur bones and the pagan altar. With pleasant cottages hugging two sides of this churchyard and a village school playground the third and with no fame or notoriety to attract the unruly, I rather hoped to find the church open. But no – although I gathered it generally is unlocked. Without even a porch for me to browse in, the bolted door seemed more reserved and unwelcoming than is usually the case.

Fortunately the leaded windows are low to the ground and the glass clear so much could be gleaned from an undignified and furtive-looking prowl around – watched I dare say by suspicious eyes from the cottages. Pevsner makes much of the Early English arcade pillars, octagonal with concave panels, and these I could see without difficulty. In one's daily life bread always tries to land on the carpet butter side down; hence, with this expectation in mind, I hardly expected my windowed gaze to land on the 16th century tombstone brass but there it was, large as life, all eighteen inches of it. There is also a lectern that looks very much like that marvellous old example of medieval woodwork at Detling and I should have liked to have had a closer look at that. Nevertheless there is no doubt that clear glass windows, conveniently placed, are a most effective substitute for access denied and a soothing salve for frustrated hopes.

Externally the church looks fine. From where I sat under a tulip tree (I hope that the characteristic leaves are recognisable in my drawing. It is a criterion of a satisfactory drawing that the trees depicted be identifiable – too often they are not as the reader of this book will doubtless confirm) the mass of the church looked rather like a battleship steaming towards the Rother levels in the west. It is the tall Perpendicular tower that gives that impression and I imagine it is this tower which is the pride of Wittersham. It is visible for miles around and possesses a large and dignified double-decker window that would grace a cathedral. The tower is topped by an elegant vane, dated 1751, which, I have read, makes it almost the oldest dated vane in Kent. I have also read that the tower provided a beacon for use in emergencies like the Armada. It is the appropriate height for such a task and, I am sure, would come high on any league table of Kent towers. I expect it is visible from the sea, ten miles or more away across the Marsh – hence the beacon.

Behind my tulip tree, I identified, to my satisfaction at any rate, a Judas tree, planted by the Men of the Trees. It is an attractive and uncommon tree but, remembering its historical or biblical association, it seems to my way of thinking an unhappy choice for a churchyard. Yews cannot be beaten in churchyards. One sees many aged specimens but rarely young ones. We are living on the foresight of our forefathers but make no provision for future generations as they did. We should.

BARHAM
St. John the Baptist

Beora's settlement

As one descends the road towards Elham from Barham Downs, where once Briton disputed (unsuccessfully) with Roman and King John mustered with an army (unnecessarily) to repel the French, the first building to greet one is Barham church, protectively placed above its village on the Nailbourne. It is no exaggeration to say that here, and in the adjoining villages along the valley, it is all quite delightful with the churches doing full justice to their surroundings.

Barham's is cruciform in plan, consisting of nave, chancel, north and south transepts, south aisle and west tower with spire. Much flint and disintegrating plaster complete a distinctly substantial edifice spanning the Early English, Decorated and Perpendicular periods with a suspicion of Norman at the base of the tower. The churchyard is spacious and open but has suffered from the unfortunate urge to clear headstones away to fence the perimeter and, less happy, to enclose the churchyard compost/rubbish heap; I can hardly imagine that such use is what the bereaved had in mind when they commissioned the memorials. There is no record of lightning damage here though to my mind the tall, copper spire does rather invite a strike and the peal of 5040 doubles in 1953 lasting almost three hours seems to me to be challenging providence. I am glad that I was not within earshot of this marathon and that providence remained patient.

Internally, the first thing to attract one's attention is the list of the 1914-18 casualties, which at Barham includes the illustrious name of Kitchener. Entering the nave, one steps up, not down as so often is the case. The modern parquet flooring is, I presume, responsible for this departure from convention. Before restoration there were galleries for choir and organ. The galleries have been swept away and the organ translated to the north transept after a brief spell in the chancel, a repeated movement that only goes to support my contention that organs are a bulky nuisance in churches never designed to accommodate them. One inevitably develops bees in one's bonnet and a prolonged exploration of country churches has engendered an antagonism to organs in mine.

The memorials are mostly concentrated in the south transept where one family holds sway – they include a Bishop of Montreal and Metropolitan of Canada amongst their number. There is also a large obelisk at the west end of the aisle and this, despite its elaboration, gets short shrift from Pevsner. Missing from the past are the head of a 14th century brass figure, the old communion plate, both stolen I believe, and the white ensign from HMS Raglan, sunk at the Dardanelles. In my opinion battle flags do become a church.

One of the assassins of Becket lived at Barham Court, beside the churchyard wall. Neither the house there now, nor this present church, were standing when the murder was committed and it is a relief to infer from their presence that the village suffered no disadvantage from its association with the crime.

162

Like its neighbour Barham, Adisham church is that comparative rarity amongst the parish churches of Kent, a cruciform construction, or so it became by the building programmes of the 14th century when transepts were added to the Norman and 12th century beginnings. Embedded in a pronounced slope, the church towers above its village and, when viewed from east of the chancel, presents a cliff-like aspect to the houses clustered below – an impression that must be heightened by the longitudinal rows of thirteen Early English lancet windows which light the three sides of the chancel.

Adisham is also rare in possessing a central tower; a much more appropriate siting than the western end of the nave. In my sketch can be seen the pyramidal cap which crowns the tower today. There is an old framed picture in the church which depicts this tower quite differently – embattled and without any spire. Apparently by 1869 the state of repair of the church had deteriorated to such an extent that a complete restoration was required, involving reroofing the chancel, removing the upper stage of the tower and substituting the pyramid.

Not surprisingly, one of the problems of a central tower which houses the bells must be the ringing arrangements, for it is inconvenient if the ringers block the aisle. There is only one place they can go – above, at the not inconsiderable height of the nave ceiling. The question then arises of how to reach the bell chamber. At Adisham they have solved the problem by the provision of a long, precarious-looking ladder leading up from the floor of the north transept; bell ringers are presumably young and agile and up to negotiating that ladder: it would not appeal to me.

From the nave, the effect of the central tower is dramatic. One is confronted, as one looks towards the chancel, by four massive, rectangular blocks of rough grey stone which together act as the piers of the tower and create the cruciform crossing. They reek of the primitive past and are well worth coming to see, making one wish that more central towers remained from the Saxon hegemony when I believe they were more the fashion architecturally.

After the visual impact of the great Norman piers which support the tower, the 13th century chancel is a let-down, made more so by the Victorian restoration which, misguidedly in my unschooled opinion, retiled the floor and lined the walls of the chancel with tiles to the level of the dado. What a pity and how unsuitable but, I suppose, how Victorian. The chancel is in fact rescued by stone coffin lids on either side of the altar. The monks of Christchurch, Canterbury had a priory next to the church and one imagines that the lids cover a pair of them.

No famous vicars have officiated here even though it is so close to Canterbury. But one, John Bland, for his obstinate refusal to recant, was economically joined with his colleague from Rolvenden at the same stake in July, 1555, and burnt. The church pamphlet finds the inclusion of the martyr in the list of vicars 'interesting'; one concludes that the lapse of time has worked its healing magic at Adisham.

WOOTTON
St. Martin

Wood farmstead

Wootton must have one of the most unassuming churches in the Kent country-side. One finds it, with difficulty, shrouded by trees and with no suggestion that it acts as the focus for its thinly spread village. The churchyard is small, the headstones largely Victorian, certainly not recent, and the trees overhang it to shut out the sun-light and confine the spirit. There is no possibility here of the tower beckoning above the tops of the trees.

It is a 14th century village church of extreme simplicity; a small nave, a smaller chancel and a modest west tower. There is a south porch, evidently Victorian, with an elaboration of ornamental woodwork, making it a challenge to draw. Indeed the whole church is an unco-operative subject mainly because the trees press in closely and prevent any all-embracing view. In these circumstances the fish-eye effect tends to become unavoidable and perspective intractable. The church is constructed of flint, reinforced by stone at the quoins and with one outsize brick buttress for the tower. It all looked to be in a good state of preservation and had been 'over-restored in 1878 by a Mr Withers'. Poor Mr Withers, what could he have done to deserve such a condemnation? I am sure that he was a respected architect, a loving husband and a kind father. Despite, or perhaps because of, his endeavours the church still retains, as reminders of past centuries, scratch dials at the foot of the tower and traces of the slope of an earlier roof.

What it was like inside I could not say – a locked door and impenetrably opaque windows prevented the slightest acquaintance with the contents; I would think that austerity would be the keynote, but perhaps there would also be a feeling of cosiness in such a diminutive building. In default of the interior, I was obliged to content myself with the porch and to deduce as much of the character of the church as I could from what I found there. The notices of varying antiquity included a state-ment of the 1985 collection for Christian Aid, a pamphlet about overseas settle-ment, a leaflet announcing a healing/medical conference, the services for September and October, the flower arranging and cleaning rosters, a certificate of Employers Liability Insurance, a photostat of an article from The Times about three parishes near Salisbury, the money raised in 1982 and 1983 for the United Society for the Propogation of the Gospel and an unintelligible notice promising free access to the Chapter House for the 'French Connection' and the 'Canterbury Walloon Congrega-tion 1575'. Altogether a curiously miscellaneous collection and I do not know what impression of the church can be derived from this catalogue, but the church is undeniably still operational.

There was in addition an appeal from the Samaritans encouraging would-be suicides to contact them. Quite frankly, I think an open church far more likely to offer comfort to the suicidally inclined.

DENTON   *Valley farmstead*
St. Mary Magdalene

I think that anyone who actually manages to find Denton church deserves a prize and I suppose that my reward was to find it open. On my map it is marked at the southern limit of the village, close by Denton Court. No sign of the church in the village but at the entrance of the drive to the invisible court was a signpost for the church. So in I ventured, cautiously of course, and with my eyes swivelling around for the church. No indication by the time I reached the mansion; still no sign after I had passed the house and halted in a cul-de-sac of converted stables and garages beyond. Back I went down the drive and on to the main road to try further south. By the time I had passed Tappington Farm, of Ingoldsby Legends fame, I realised that I was growing cold, not warm. Back to the drive where by good fortune I found a farm worker setting out for his tractor. Yes, the church was here all right; across the field of stubble and hidden in a dense clump of trees – part of the Denton Court estate, he said, but I was welcome to park in the drive and go up to the church. I should never have found the building without local knowledge.

Up the grassy path through the stubble I went accompanied by the put-put of the tractor and the coughing of pheasants only to find when I had reached the iron gate to the churchyard that I had forgotten my spectacles and had to go back and repeat the process. The church is entirely enclosed by trees and only becomes visible through the branches at the gate. As the young man observed, it could become quite spooky after dark. Very like its neighbour, Wootton, it is small, uncomplicated Early English, with nave, chancel and plain west tower – but with battlements here, in deference to the Court, no doubt. As with Wootton, the press of trees makes a complete composition impossible but, one hopes, the impression of rustic simplicity can be conveyed.

A small porch shelters the north doorway which is scored with the cabbalistic marks of masons and what are reputed to be pilgrims' crosses. Inconspicuous they are; presumably they were made with the same knife that the pilgrim used for his food and for his protection – he would not be too anxious to spoil its edge or blunt its point on the unyielding stone. The micro-nave is unremarkable apart from an enigmatic stone cross let into the wall beside the pulpit. Inscribed with lettering that is neither Roman nor Greek, in M.R. James' world it would be runic and haunted; entirely appropriate for a church and setting that cry out for a ghost story. In the chancel I found myself standing on a ledger stone which read in an elegantly carved inscription below the regulation coat of arms – 'Reader beware: Lest you inadvertently: Trample upon Sacred Ashes: You stand at the Stone of Y^e late: Revd Edwd LUNN AM:' Oh dear! However I was reassured to notice that the parson's stall also rested on the stone. Despite being commemorative, ledger stones must, by their nature, expect to be trodden on and so I think the Rev. Edward was being a shade unreasonable.

Apparently Thomas Gray is known to have visited Denton. From this premise, Charles Igglesden concluded in 1932 that Denton may have been in the poet's mind when he wrote his elegy. Nice to think so, at any rate.

168

Bicknor must be one of the most unusual churches in Kent, if not the country, and also one of the most deceptive. If one found it in the suburbs of any town, I doubt if one would give it a second glance. Commonplace Victorian it would seem. Unweathered walls of flint chippings; neat undefaced windows; a good slate roof that reaches down on both sides of the nave like a catslide; a south west tower with circular bell openings; a porch that is plain to a degree — together they make a picture of Victorian architecture and one which is pure camouflage.

The rural setting must first arouse one's curiosity. Surrounded on all sides by orchards, the church stands in the middle of an immense fruit farm. There is no village and no obstacle to separate orchard from churchyard — just a ring of yews, pines and sycamores and beyond, the endless ranks of apple trees. Why should anybody build a church here? Alternatively why should they abandon a church here? The plague?

The first surprise was to find the door unlocked. To judge from the cobwebs on the lock mechanism, the church is never locked. The second surprise was to be accosted by a voice from the gloom within — there is no artificial lighting whatsoever. The voice belonged to a cyclist, thirtyish, who comes up to this church on the Downs from Rainham from time to time for peace and quiet. One tends to feel wary of such individuals but my companion proved to be amiable and informative and together we toured the interior of this remarkable little church. What makes this church one of only two similar in the country, said my informant, is the use of chalk as the building material. Chalk does not look very robust or permanent and is, I gathered, vulnerable to the combination of frost and damp. In fact in a particularly hard winter in the 1860s the chalk began to fail and a drastic rebuilding became necessary culminating in the construction of an external carapace of flint which is what gives the Victorian impression. But apart from the shell and vitreous floor tiles there is hardly a trace of Victoriana — it is Norman work which predominates inside; a blocked west doorway and four great rectangular piers below the semi-circular arches which form the arcades to the minimal north and south aisles. The smooth chalk walls are bare of enrichment and free of memorials and the benches primitive and few. There are in fact only three memorials in the church — in the vestry a tablet to a vicar's daughter dated 1676, a brass statement attached to the garish reredos and, at the base of the tower, an anonymous stone coffin lid. There is an air of rustic simplicity and poverty which all the fittings, or lack of them, confirm. Only the marble font is grandiose — a contradiction like the outside.

Surrounded as it is by acres of orchards, the church must normally be a lonely place but not in October at apple picking time with pop music filling the air.

IVYCHURCH
St. George

Ivy covered church

More or less in the centre of Romney Marsh, Ivychurch is of an appropriate stature to act as the hub around which revolve the other thirteen churches, not to mention those which have already disintegrated. Why they are all here is difficult to explain in terms of today's, or even yesterday's, population. My theory, for the little it is worth, is that they were built in the early centuries after the Norman conquest when the Marsh was not reliably consolidated and church building was the Church's way of defying the sea and invoking the support of the Almighty. Others will have more convincing hypotheses.

Built on the foundations of an earlier version, 14th century Ivychurch does admirable justice to its pivotal role. It is undoubtedly large; a fine landmark of a west tower, a double-decker vaulted porch and a long nave, flanked by equally long aisles, all three leading without interruption into chancel and chapels; plus two stair turrets; together these combine to make a church worthy of any town, not just a scattered hamlet. There is a great air of spaciousness here — only a few defeated-looking chairs to occupy a nave once filled by painted box pews. And birds; they seem to have taken over the interior and will be a problem to evict from the lofty ceilings. A cat could not do it but a hawk might. The floor everywhere is good — warm red pre-Victorian tiles and I would have guessed, wrongly, that the church has so far been spared restoration. There are no monuments, just one ledger stone and one grey, unmarked slab. One supposes that the church has always exceeded demand and has never enjoyed the patronage of gentry worthy of being immortalised within its walls. What a pity that better use could not have been made of this beautiful stone shell. It deserves, at least, a chest-tomb, a knight and his lady, surrounded by 'weepers' and decorated by coats of arms and, for the gangways, to be floored by ranks of ledger stones — the whole illuminated by shafts of the sunlight which floods through the splendid clear glass windows. All that is except the Perpendicular window at the east end of the north chapel, blocked presumably for the same reason that the north aisle has been partitioned off. Contemplating this empty expanse of grey walls and brick-red tiles I was reminded of a stable yard; my self-esteem was consequently considerably flattered to read in Arthur Mee, on return home, that the roughness of the floor tiles is said to be due to the hooves of horses.

The favoured direction for a view of Ivychurch is from the east from whence the end trio of Perpendicular windows can be seen to best advantage. To obtain a reasonable perspective one must trespass on the adjoining fields, as I imagine many have discovered before me. When I was there an elderly man and his two boxers were exercising themselves but he very accommodatingly, and not for the first time I am sure, agreed to withdraw so that a sketch could be made from the middle of his paddock. He was, it transpired, a dog breeder and his willingness to accept yet another church fancier on his land was only mitigated by his parting remark — 'I hope my dogs don't see you off. That's what they are for'. Defenceless in his paddock, so did I — and my sketch was completed in record time.

NEWCHURCH
St. Peter and St. Paul

New – as on the site of the old church

Before exploring the church here, I had a sustaining ploughman's lunch at the pub, the Black Bull. There I saw an aerial photograph of the hamlet in which the shadow of the wartime runway is clearly visible. An engraved brass plate below the picture states that, in June, July, August and September, 1944, three squadrons of RAF fighters, operating from this ghostly strip, destroyed 638 flying bombs. A super achievement and how annoying for the German High Command to find that their precious V1s were being swatted like flies as they crossed the coast. It is a record that the RAF and this village have every reason to be proud of, and the people of Kent to be thankful for, and, although not strictly speaking concerned with the church, I cannot resist including it. I am sure, anyway, that the church tower was a welcome navigational aid for the returning fighters.

So to come to the church; the most obvious comment is 'how typical of this country still to call 'New' a church that has existed for seven hundred years'. It stands in its churchyard surrounded by sycamores and ivy-clad willows and moated by a watery ditch. The relatively high water table in the Marsh must account for the instability of the foundations; the tilt of the tower is quite perceptible despite strenuous efforts to preserve its integrity. Not only is it out of the vertical but it also appears to have developed a dog leg at the upper stage, but these idiosyncracies make it all the more endearing and the designation 'New' more enjoyable.

Like all the Marsh churches, and indeed most village churches, Newchurch must be quite out of proportion to the needs of its parishioners. For the existing church-goers here, not that I know anything about them, the derelict old school house, for that is what I think it was, would be ample in terms of dimensions. In fact this building, run down though it is today, still bears, as I thought, the unmistakable signature of medieval architecture. They had a more ambitious idea of worship in the Middle Ages and, however superfluous their churches may be today and perhaps were in the past, what marvellous gestures of faith and aspiration we have inherited. Newchurch is a remote example of this optimism and, like many others, is much to be admired. As always, it is the aesthetic focus of its immediate surroundings; never do these old churches clash, in the way modern buildings often do, with the countryside around.

If I might belatedly summarise the characteristics of this church – it was locked, with padlock and chain, no less. I could peer inside by balancing precariously on my chair and the little I made out did not seem particularly elaborate. To be frank, what most forcibly impressed me were the two label stops (ie the ornamental bosses) at the ends of the drip stone over the south porch door. These are two deeply cut spheres of oak leaves that one might more usually have expected to find in the interior. If such a relatively unimportant feature of the church as the porch entrance door bears work of this quality what can I have missed inside? My notes say that I observed a nave, two aisles, two chapels and screens but what decorated, or was commemorated in, these sealed interiors, I do not suppose I shall ever know.

JAS

LITTLEBOURNE
St. Vincent

Little stream

The expansion of the village in the 1960s has now rather invalidated any claim of St. Vincent's to be a country church and I was a trifle disappointed to find it so closely beset by the 20th century. Nevertheless, first impressions are often misleading and Littlebourne is no exception. The first thing to attract one's attention is the immense barn running along the western perimeter of the churchyard (Pevsner suggests that it was the grange of the monks of St. Augustine's abbey at Canterbury in the 14th century) and, next, on a smaller scale, the tortured, twisting weeping spruce, propped upright by a timber support, beside the lychgate. The churchyard as a whole improves on inspection and is well stocked with mellow old tombstones and appropriate yews. The latter do obstruct a decent view of the church, but any yew is better than no yew. Every diocese should maintain a nursery for replacement yews but I doubt if they do.

In appearance, as one approaches up the churchyard path, the church certainly does not reflect its age, 13th century. The walls on the south side look to have been restored; the flints are in such good condition and so closely laid in regular courses. The north side (my view), less subject to the public gaze, has been allowed to deteriorate and weather, so it seems. In fact, some repairs must have been carried out; Pevsner reports that the north aisle fell down about 1800 and was only partly replaced. Evidence of this catastrophe can be found in a blocked arcade and by the substitution of an inferior timber post for a stone arcade pillar. Only an expert would detect the collapse from the outside; I certainly did not from where I sat. Perhaps my attention was distracted by the wording on many of the headstones – 'Here lies X, wife (or son or daughter) of the above Y', Y being inscribed below X and not above as stated. It seemed an intriguing contradiction but there must be some rational explanation.

It was a relatively mild day at the end of October when I drew this church but I have rarely felt so cold when inside. The chill got to me in less than five minutes so I wonder how the congregation manages. One notices that the rectangular piers which divide the south aisle from the nave are no longer vertical – possibly the south aisle could go the way of the north aisle. Another interesting feature stems from the roof. Viewed from the churchyard, it is obvious that the ridge of the chancel roof is considerably higher than that of the nave (an indication of 13th century rebuilding says Pevsner); seen from inside, the step has been lost and the ceilings of each appear of similar height. From a decorative point of view, the church displays more stained glass than most and, when the sun shines, the effect must be dazzling. There are of course a great many windows to accommodate all this stained glass, eleven lancets in the chancel alone. The chancel is otherwise bare of adornment so the diffused light from the windows must go some way to make good the austerity. For a parish in what is almost a suburb of Canterbury, such lack of enrichment is unexpected – particularly in one that once provisioned the monks of St. Augustine.

ICKHAM
St. John the Evangelist

I do not think that there are many parish churches in Kent that can have such an arresting effect on the newcomer as does Ickham's. Set well back from the village street by a broad sweep of grass, the church acts as a medieval backdrop to the trees of Ickham Hall on one side and to a long range of black, timbered barns on the other. One cannot easily pass it by and nor would I want to. It makes a picture that one would describe as 'chocolate box' were it not a reality. The colours deserve a painter, not a sketcher in black and white, and I am sure there are plenty of the former each summer.

The once navigable approaches to Canterbury from the sea have attracted an outstanding crop of 13th and 14th century churches — Littlebourne, Wickhambreaux and Ickham are all within sight of each other in this low-lying belt, watered by the Nailbourne stream; Fordwich and Sturry are not far away on the Stour, and one can understand why this fertile plain was one of the favoured granaries of the monks of Canterbury. They knew what was good for them and they left us these works of art to mark their appreciation. The churches are all handsome and Ickham stands comparison with any. It is particularly easy to interpret for there is inside a meticulous framed plan and explanation of the architectural features. From this one learns that one of the rectors was Edmund Cranmer, brother of Thomas, deprived of his living in Queen Mary's reign; not guilt by association as one might expect but for the less dangerous sin of marriage. Another incumbent, two centuries earlier, had a more fortunate career and survived to become Chancellor of Oxford University. As well as the illustrated plan, on the same pier there is an architect's elevation in colour; in 1825 the tower was neatly battlemented with an inset spire. Pevsner says there were 'extensive repairs in 1845' and that presumably was when the present overblown and out-of-scale spire was installed.

There are two transepts here, each containing a recessed chest-tomb with recumbent stone figures. In the north transept we find our friend the chancellor; in the south a one-time lord of the manor and warrior, Thomas de Baa. He, appropriately for his status, lies in full armour. Since his occupation was, primarily, fighting and his situation depended on his prowess in arms as much as on anything else, it seems entirely right that he should be so remembered. In point of fact, I cannot remember seeing any effigies of medieval knights who are not in full armour. Romantic they now look but very impressive they must have been when properly painted as I am sure they were.

When I recently 'did' Ivychurch, I was only too conscious of the birds that lived within and it appeared to me, then, that the only way to evict the intruders was by employing a hawk. Here at Ickham they have a better solution. On the cleared floor of the north transept there lay a bird cage, baited with seed, in which birds are trapped to be released unharmed in the churchyard later. It is true there were no birds in the cage but then neither were there any in the church. Only me.

It is not beyond the bounds of credibility that Wingham might by now be a university town like Oxford or Cambridge for that is what could have been in the archiepiscopal minds when they founded, in the 13th century, a collegiate church here and provided for a provost and six canons. I always find it surprising that it took Canterbury until the 20th century to achieve the status of a university city; it should have led the way and Wingham might have been the instrument. The collegiate church survived to exercise its function until 1547 when Thomas Cromwell's plans for the suppression of the collegiate churches and the confiscation of their revenues finally caught up with Wingham and the unlucky Edmund Cranmer found himself the last in a long, distinguished line of provosts (the confiscation did Cromwell no good, as we know, for he lost his head in the end). The outcome today is a handsome parish church of flint and stone, still large despite the loss through neglect of the north aisle. Set in the middle of its attractively medieval village, it could be said to be too attractive for its comfort, unless of course one is part of the tourist industry.

My sketch cannot find room for the needle spire on top of the 14th century west tower. One would need to make use of the first floor of the old canonry across the road to do full justice to the overall dimensions of this church which, from the south, presents a sunlit assembly of patterned buttresses, double-decker porch and clustered tombstones; on the sunless, unregarded north, the absent aisle and blocked arches tell of the unmaintained ambitions of the founders. On a more topical level, I was intrigued to read in the porch a letter from the local M.P. demonstrating his somewhat ambivalent attitude to Sunday trading – in response, no doubt, to some special pleading by the vicar.

A fine and spacious interior is what one might expect from a church with such antecedents and this is what one finds. An extra-large chancel (to accommodate the canons?) reveals the outlines of stolen brasses on the tomb slabs of long-dead provosts of the college with, on either side, a chapel devoted to the memory of prominent members of the laity. In the south chapel, the Oxendens made sure of their immortality by both statuary and a painted frieze of shields in which the ox figures frequently as a pun on their name. Sadly, the last of the family, who contributed to the elegant chapel railings, died in the 1920s. I can never understand how these populous families become extinct but vanish they do. In the north chapel, if one could see it properly, one would find the recumbent figures of members of the Palmer family which entertained Elizabeth I when she complained about the state of the church.

Elizabeth's visitation saved the church but not its original glory. Apart from the north aisle, never restored, the main feature of the medieval repairs is the set of arcade pillars. As at Littlebourne, economy exerted its unwelcome pressure and timber was used rather than stone. Five huge chestnut trunks and one oak now support the roof. They have been there over four hundred years and the parent trees must have been three hundred years a-growing when felled. Wood that has lasted for seven hundred years or so cannot be all that inferior to stone.

Elmstone really is the back of beyond, a situation which must be very much to the liking of the owners of the houses scattered thinly round about. It is the type of place where one is liable to pass a house that one covets and its remoteness on the mainland fringe of the Stour marshes should ensure that it stays firmly off the beaten track, undefiled by progress. Aelvetone, Ealmestone, Elmestone, Elmerstone and now Elmstone constitute a surfeit of spellings for the simple hamlet that was recorded in the Domesday Book. The church stands at a crossroads, where so little passes that I could confidently establish my chair on the highway; fields and paddocks surround, occupied only by grazing hunters with the houses that own them discreetly screened by trees in the background. The church was here long before them and they do not press it too closely.

It is a straight-forward flint building of early Norman ancestry, possessed of a severely flat-topped west tower, nave, aisle and chancel. The particular attributes which confirm its provenance, so I learnt, are the jambs of the tiny Norman windows. It has long been standard architectural practice to strengthen vertical edges with dressed stone, however primitive, but at Elmstone the jambs of the windows were too early to qualify for dressed stone and the vertical faces end in untrammelled rough old flints. I cannot consciously remember having seen windows like this before and that fact must give Elmstone a special place in my pantheon of medieval churches in Kent. Another market here is an elaborate headstone beside the porch, elegantly carved and still legible despite a date of 1562; like the 'undressed' windows, this date grants the headstone a respectable place in any batting order.

When I attempted to open the porch door, I was somewhat startled to hear a voice from within call out – 'other door'. To be honest I hardly expected to find Elmstone unlocked and I doubt if it normally is. However, by good fortune, two electricians were inside rewiring the church – an expenditure as eccentric as it is surprising in a tiny, geographically peripheral, Norman church. I wonder if it is those windows that guarantee Elmstone a privileged place in the care and maintenance stakes.

The cosy, unsophisticated interior is enlivened by the surviving screen, a self-confident hanging monument in the chancel and, in a cleared space in the nave, a substantial font. It is said to be Norman also and certainly looks it. This is a dear little church of a size appropriate to the likely congregation in the past and in the present, but perhaps over-optimistic for the future. Only one thing puzzled me – there is no ladder or other method of access to the upper chamber of the tower. The electricians had their own ladder, but clearly that ladder would leave with them. What is the point of a tower if no-one can ascend it? I expect Elmstone conceals the answer somewhere – it is just another of the idiosyncracies, like the Norman windows, that makes this sturdy little church such an enchanting and unusual find on the edges of Kent proper.

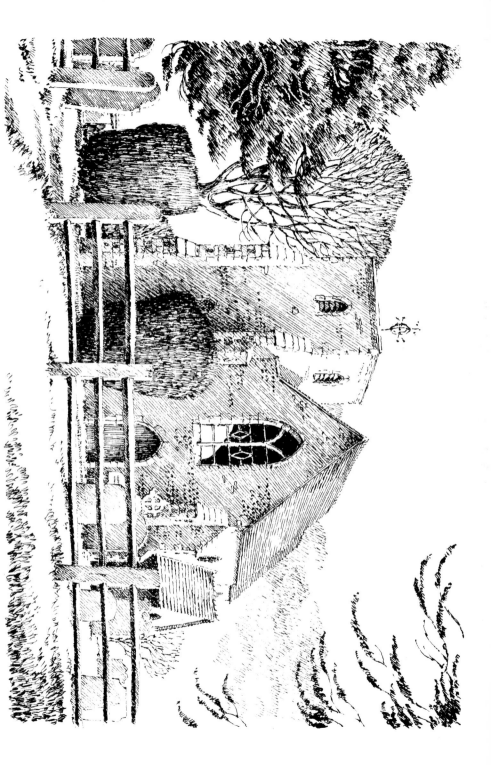

Womenswold church, or Wymenswold as the rural deanery of East Bridge has it, stands on a grassy mound surrounded by the attractive 18th century houses of its hamlet. Not far away is the Kent colliery of Snowdown and I had rather hoped to be able to include the silhouette of the winding gear as a backdrop to the church, but geography was against me.

The church rests on its knoll, unfenced and wall-less. For a hamlet so small and innocent-looking as Womenswold any form of boundary wall seems superfluous and the church here is thus happily positioned on its plinth in the centre of its tiny parish. There is not a great deal to see externally; a long, low, red roof under which chancel gives way to nave without interruption and nave is brought to a halt by the square, unbuttressed flint tower, all of which are of the Early English period. At least, that is what the lancet windows said to me, though Pevsner says the coursing of the flints in the nave suggests Norman walling. Even if I had known what to look for I doubt if I would have spotted it as the south face is, or was, covered in some form of crumbling cement rendering. I did not linger on the north side where all is dark and neglected in contrast to the open, sunlit and cared-for southern approach. This is where the tombstones lie; the northern strip of churchyard looks as if it has always been ostracised.

It was a Saturday morning in November when I arrived to explore and sketch the church and I was a little disappointed to find the door firmly locked with no hint of the whereabouts of the key. There are inside, I understand, three 18th century hanging monuments, an obelisk and tomb recesses on either side of the chancel, so it would appear that the interior is as rich in decoration as the outside walls are barren. That makes the locked door all the more frustrating though one should, of course, never allow oneself to become provoked because these precautions are all taken with the best of intentions. On the other hand, the church is so exposed to the public gaze with virtually no cover for miscreants and narrow lanes to sabotage a rapid getaway, that I cannot believe the church is vulnerable to vandalism.

Womenswold lies in a belt of glorious country only a few miles inland from Deal. Obviously there were sound geological reasons for looking for coal here and coal there is to be extracted, if the will exists. The will seems to have evaporated now, but the traces of exploitation will long remain to remind us of an activity that seems incongruous in such a pastoral landscape. Some may argue that harvesting the earth's resources underground is only different in degree from harvesting them on the surface and I suppose that is so. One activity, though, improves the land; the other disturbs it in what appears an alien, non-renewable way and I, for one, selfishly prefer the surface activity. It is the one to which the country churches are so admirably suited.

BARFRESTON
St. Nicholas

Beornfrid's farmstead

I had long postponed my visit to Barfreston church fearing it might prove a disappointment and that it would be difficult to draw. In the event, I found that it does not exactly lend itself to composition but, on the other hand, it far exceeded my expectations. It is to other village churches as the kingfisher is to other birds — in a class by itself. When it is my turn to give the dog, Boy, his daily walk and I make a rare sighting of the kingfisher that lives beside the Hadlow stream, my whole day is brightened; Barfreston church had precisely the same effect, only more so. It seemed un-English, like an exotic temple stolen from ancient Rome or Byzantium and hidden down here in the quiet Kent countryside for safe keeping.

Very small, it is just two attached rectangular boxes of flint and Norman stone from Caen. It is the enrichment of the stone, both inside and out, that transforms this church into something special. There is hardly a book about English village churches that does not discuss Barfreston, so I feel a proper caution in attempting a description. The south door alone merits, and receives, pages of learned admiration and analysis. Eight hundred years old, but clearly recognisable, are the stone portraits that make up the semi-circular arches of the doorway: the Norman foot soldier, the lady of fashion, the resting workman and so on and, amongst the symbolic carvings, the monkey riding on the back of a goat and others more suited to the medieval mind. I have never seen anything to compare — except perhaps in cathedrals. Tiny Norman windows light the interior and between them blind arcades decorate the exterior surfaces — to economise in stone, it is said. The effect is so sumptuous that I cannot believe that it is the product of anything so prosaic as economy.

My arrival was attended by mixed fortune to start with. Not a soul about — good; but the famous south door held fast — less good. Later, as I was completing my sketch from the roadside below the church, a young lad approached to inspect progress. He proved to be an enthusiastic guide. First we went to the cottage of the lady who keeps the key, 'the door was open', she said, 'as it always is. Try again.' Back to the church went young Morgan and I, to inspect the interior under his knowledgeable guidance. He showed me what was what, down to the string that operates the bell in the yew tree outside, while I listened respectfully. Back again to the lady custodian for the church pamphlet (eighth edition) and a present of her son-in-law's erudite architectural notes. I hope it will not sound patronising if I say that those I met here, including the landlord of the pub, were a credit to their marvellous little church.

When Barfreston was saved from decay in 1840, the porch over the south doorway was removed. Architecturally inappropriate it may have been, but without its protection we should not have that stunning carving to marvel at today.

Otterden church appears not so much a church as a monument to 18th century eccentricity and privilege and quite exceptional it all is too. Unless one has the invaluable Pevsner on one's shelves or a gazetteer of Kent's churches one would never be aware of the existence of this church. There is no village now — there must have been one once, I suppose, for there are scattered headstones in the long, wet grass of the diminutive churchyard — but there is a mansion, Otterden Place. One cannot see the church from the lane so one just has to pluck up courage and press on down the tree-lined drive through the park towards the Place. After two or three hundred yards one arrives at the battlemented screen that separates the house from the park and its livestock. Immediately to the right of the gateway, and behind a low flint wall, one finds a church that looks more like a Georgian summer house or orangery than a place of worship.

The church was built in the 1750s on the foundations of a small medieval church; the designer of and subscriber to this replacement church was the then owner of Otterden Place, which he also rebuilt, I infer. I cannot conceive that he took advice from anyone or allowed tradition to influence him. So he built what he liked — in this case an uncompromising rectangle of red brick, pierced at regular intervals by classical windows and edged by smoothly rusticated stonework, the whole covered by a shallow, over-hanging slate roof. A small protruding appendix at the chancel end was given buttresses to convey the ecclesiastical impression, but it does not succeed — the building looks elegant but it does not resemble a church. I do not suppose, though, that there was anyone in the 1750s in a position to object to the Rev. Granville Wheler's designs or intentions so we now have an unusual and charming monument to one man's idiosyncracies and independence.

The church was locked. Very likely it almost always is. I should like to have seen the inside, but there was no-one about for me to accost and, despite a Union Jack at the masthead of Otterden Place, no-one answered the front door bell. I think they were all out shooting as there were constant noises off. Since it is the individual creation of a wealthy cleric, I expect the unadorned interior contains hidden riches; for instance Pevsner says that the pews have 'Chinese Chippendale pierced backs' and from that the standard of the rest can be inferred. There are some very grand medieval monuments relating to the 1400s and 1500s and their presence does raise a question in one's mind. They obviously existed in the original church; were they removed and stored during the reconstruction or was Wheler's revision built around them without disturbing anything below? One may be confident, at any rate, that an interior well worth seeing lies behind those impenetrable red-brick walls.

Late November is an unpromising time of year in which to sketch in the open and 1985 provided a particularly unpleasant specimen. The North Downs offer an exceptionally attractive countryside and it is always a pleasure to explore the churches there. In poor weather, though, the low cloud clings to the plateau and it felt, at Otterden, as if I was drawing under water — cold water.

Eastling church is better inside than out, especially on a cold November day. Externally it looks vaguely Victorian which, of course, it is not. I think it could be the pyramid spire on top of the heavily buttressed tower which gives this impression, or maybe the west porch is responsible. Fortunately for the churchgoers the incongruity of the porch is largely concealed by that magnificent old yew, contemporary it is said with the Norman doorway, and very obviously still full of vigour.

Once through the porch the antiquity of this 13th century church becomes more apparent. First, naturally, there is the Norman doorway, then there is the stone-flagged floor and the stone seating along the south wall, for the 'weakest', supplemented in a softer age by commodious box pews. A teasing riddle is the unexplained row of arches behind the choir stalls. There are four of these and they looked to me like the canopies of sedilia without the seating. They cannot have been intended for that purpose for there are completed sedilia on the south side of the chancel where they are normally to be found. Pevsner claims to be as baffled as is the church's information board; someone must know the answer.

The south chapel has been stripped of pews, ostensibly to accommodate a bulky organ which does nothing for the architecture and is surely not what the James family intended when they commissioned their family monument in 1592. Here we see the patriarch and lord of six thousand five hundred acres and several manors hereabouts, with his wife and kneeling pairs of sons and daughters. The offspring diminish as they recede from their parents, but they are identically portrayed, the boys in the regulation armour of an Elizabethan gentleman, ready, I assume, to repel the Spanish invasion. One might have expected the sculptor to make the children look like children, but this was not the convention. At any rate, both generations of the family are generously remembered in the James' exhuberant obituary.

'Grossly over-restored by R.C. Hussey (as usual) in 1856' says Pevsner and this may explain the misleading external look of the church. It is a discouraging fact that well-meant and necessary restoration (there was, to be true, a fire at Eastling prior to Mr Hussey's work) often seems to cast a blight on its victim. I much prefer to see stonework gently crumbling under the influence of the weather. When it becomes too degraded to retain its strength, the repairs ought to be undertaken with a different material, say brick, rather than replaced with unmellowed stone. Bricks amongst stonework never look out of place: instead they seem to add character. For instance, the south-eastern buttress of the tower, here solidly of brick, harmonises entirely with the remaining two. Other churches similarly reinforced by brickwork come to mind — West Stourmouth and Elmsted — both enhanced in appearance and improved in stability, no doubt. On the other hand, how lucky we are that reinforced concrete and steel girders were not available when the Victorians performed their rescue acts. Modern materials may be cheaper, but they certainly jar — better a genuine ruin.

Staple church lies closely parallel to the road that runs through the village but, luckily for the church and village, it is a road that runs to nowhere in particular in the hinterland behind Deal. One cannot help noticing as one drives around the countryside here that they have grubbed out most of the hedges. As a practice, the removal of hedges is invariably criticised by conservationists; I find it somehow liberating and the wide-open, sweeping fields around Staple look marvellous, if windy. Possibly they are better to admire than to live amongst.

Very conveniently, the key of the church is kept immediately across the road from the old lych-gate. The lady from whom I retrieved it was most helpful; care of the church must now be the mainspring of her and her husband's lives — as drawing them now is of mine. She sold me a copy of the church's excellent detailed pamphlet; he winds the rare, one-handed clock daily and together they keep an eye on the church's well-being. Not that it is neglected. The Friends of Kent Churches are currently contributing to its repairs and the neighbouring parishes have rallied round and cleared up the churchyard which currently looks a trifle shaven, but doubtless it will recover.

The long level church spans four centuries of building, from the hidden Saxon window, through Norman and Early English, to the Perpendicular north aisle — plus the inevitable Victorian porch. The walls are of rough, unknapped flints and look their age, especially near the little low window with its scratch dial on the south side of the chancel. The other windows and buttresses are immaculate, after restoration, but time and financial stringency will cure that.

When one enters the church, down a step, one is confronted by what must be one of the most elaborate fonts in Kent. It is substantial, comprehensively carved and documented at length. Sculpted around the bowl are the four evangelists — Matthew with his angel, Mark his lion, Luke his ox and John his eagle — also of course the patron saint with his pilgrim's staff and scallop shell — it is an education in stone. After the splendour of the font, it is a little disappointing to find the north aisle curtained off as a reservation for the Sunday school and parochial meetings. It is the north aisle and north chapel, though, which most reward inspection for here, competing with the organ and impedimenta of the vestry, are the best memorials — virtually indeed the only ones.

One cannot leave Staple church without a mention of the lych-gate — reputed to be some five hundred years old. It is spare and elegant and the timbers have developed that wonderful soft bloom that goes with antiquity. It is right on the road but, fortunately, for most of those five hundred years there was little traffic or petrol fumes to disturb it.

As this book and its predecessor are such personal accounts of one individual's reaction to the country churches in Kent, I hope I may be forgiven for recording that it was on the day after I had explored Staple that my daughter announced her engagement. Staple church will remain etched in my memory for that reason alone, if for none other.

GOODNESTONE (by Wingham)
Holy Cross

Godwine's farmstead

There cannot be many villages like Goodnestone remaining in Kent. Built largely as an estate village, it has remained one to the present day, or so they said in the pleasant, un-done-up pub beside the church, the FitzWalter Arms. Most of the houses that line the street that leads to Goodnestone Park bear the round-headed windows of the estate and are still in its ownership. As a result there is a distinct air of coherence and timelessness in the village to which a twice-weekly bus service is unlikely to disturb.

I was very lucky in the people I met after drawing the church. Taken by the cottager who minds the bell staircase to see the sacristan-cum-verger who keeps the key, I was enthusiastically plied with information by both ladies. It is always a pleasure to look over a church in the company of the knowledgeable and here the verger has been involved with the church for over thirty years, I understand.

To start with the churchyard, one sees by the path an area of rough grass labelled 'Wild Flower Conservation Area' and there is in the porch, in corroboration, a list of thirty-four varieties found there. Then the church – 12th century in origin, it is noteworthy for an outstanding rebuilding of the nave and chancel in 1840; this gives the church a split personality – medieval tower and north side, high-quality Victorian replacement for the chancel and south side. One cannot help admiring here the orderly rows of close-set, square, knapped flints, diminishing in size with height. To my mind, these flints redeem the reconstruction and one hopes that the masons concerned left their signatures on their work. I would have.

Inside, my guided tour took me to the north chapel with its brasses on the floor. It is worth remarking that the memorials of north chapels do seem to have survived restoration and usage better on average than those in the more frequented parts of a church. Given the chance, the north side is where I would want to be. When Mr Hussey so comprehensively rebuilt the south walls of the nave and chancel, he left the interior unchanged, apart from designing a matching pulpit and font. In the vestry I was shown a framed seating plan of those days in which the pews all faced south across the nave, with his lordship's pew prominent. Presumably it was in this pew that Jane Austen sat when she came to stay; unlike the House of Commons, there appeared to be no provision for 'distinguished visitors'. According to my informants, Goodnestone remained a 'prayer book' church until 1910 when all the pews were turned round with the altar as the focus of attention rather than the pulpit. One can imagine the debates in the parochial council and the fiats from the Park which accompanied such a radical change of lay-out and service. At least the rest of the village, apart from the addition of some council housing, remains unaltered – a survivor from a past that we can hardly visualise today.

When we eventually locked up and left this remarkable, hybrid church, two pheasants crossed the churchyard path behind us, heading towards the FitzWalter Arms. Goodnestone – church and village – is that sort of place.

---

* In restoring this church, Hussey was advised by, I gather, the celebrated Mr Rickman who invented the descriptive terms Early English, Decorated and Perpendicular. I expect the latter architect was a restraining influence on the former.

What a disappointment. Here is a sumptuous church with modern surroundings that fail to complement its grandeur or antiquity, spoil it even. Old Romney, not far away and much more modest with its dykes, willows and sheep, seems to me infinitely preferable. But then perhaps I was prejudiced by the notice on the church door – 'Open out of Service Hours 9 to 12'; not on Wednesday in my experience and I nearly left in high dudgeon.

One cannot leave St. Nicholas' tower, though, in a bad temper. I had read, in advance of my visit, how in the 12th century it was bonded to the west end of the Norman church, thus making a base of arches, blind arcades and blocked windows. This would have been fascinating to see, but the doors were locked. The outside, however, bears examination and, if it had not been right on the street, continually passed by townspeople too familiar with the building to spare it a glance, I would have liked to have attempted a sketch of this tower. There are broad, shallow buttresses which are rather like a cross between primitive pilasters and the conventional buttresses of a later date and put one in mind of Brook. There are five stages – enriched with more blind arcades in the lower two, Early English in the upper two and some thing in-between in the middle stage. There is a west doorway of tiered, carved arches that almost stands comparison with the doorway at Barfreston, pinnacles at the top and the stump of a spire as the crown. This stump is variously described as all that remains of a demolished spire or all that they managed to erect before stopping work. I incline to the former theory; I cannot imagine that anyone in the Middle Ages would have had the temerity not to complete anything once begun on this splendid tower. Most books about county parish churches contain a useful list of those of particular merit or interest; of the four which I have that do this, only one mentions New Romney and then it is the celebrated east end of three gables which is extolled. I would have thought it qualified for inclusion on grounds of the tower alone. The experts think otherwise.

I wish I could have seen the interior without having to peer through the lean-to aisle windows on the south side of the tower. Through the clear glass one could make out fairly easily the Norman pillars with their distinctive square, scalloped capitals and glimpse the rows of box pews. Standing on tip-toe on the churchyard grass it becomes apparent how far below ground level lies the stone-flagged floor of the church. New Romney is about a mile from the sea and, in the reign of Edward I, the sea came in, flooded the church, and built up the ground around with shingle. It is said that the stain on the lowest few feet of the pillars marks the level reached by the sea's transgression. However, New Romney was one of the original Cinque Ports and the townspeople were not to be deterred by the sea on which their prosperity depended so it was in the next reign, the unfortunate Edward II's, that the east end was rebuilt and extended. The sea as we know had its way in the end; New Romney is no longer a seaport and, of the five churches that once served the town, only St. Nicholas' remains. One could not hope for a finer survivor – but I wish they would not lock it up.

The first thing to strike one about Lydd church is the tower. Solid and tall, it looks like a tower from the West Country, but in fact the first 80 feet were the work of one of the Canterbury masons. It now stands 132 feet high, the 50 foot extension having been added when Wolsey had the living. At the time he was planning Henry VIII's abortive military excursion to France and manoeuvring for the See of York, so I do not expect he had much time to spare for Lydd. No doubt the lady verger was correct when she said that he paid someone to do his work here. Still, he probably did authorise the increase in the tower – one of his better actions, one might say.

The church was locked when I arrived but, to compensate, the churchyard and its lyddite (I could not resist that) surroundings are most agreeable and no penance to potter in. The church has Saxon stonework to which I attributed a tiny window with a quoinless outward splay and a few courses of small, flat stones at the western end of the north aisle. What I would never have realised was that the chancel was rebuilt in the 1950s – it had been demolished by a German bomb. In my examination I felt rather like a latter day Ruskin, he who wrote so knowingly about and drew so well the stones of Italy; what a pity he did not do the same thing for the stones of England.

In due course, after a frigid hour during which I had completed my sketch, I found that a funeral was impending and that the church had been opened. I thus had a brief opportunity to view the interior before the service, for which I was very grateful. I was also grateful to the helpful verger who made sure that I took in the salient points of the church in the time available. To start with the framed plan of the church which shows very clearly where the Saxon church stood, where its Norman successor followed and how both are embraced by the Early English survivor. The 5th century Saxons are represented by a jumble of dark stones and blocked windows, the Normans by the round arcade pillars and the 20th century by the harmonious chancel; fifteen hundred years of history with not too much modernisation, I am glad to say. I found the Norman pillars particularly rewarding, having recently read that the practice was to build them up with circular stone drums, either whole or semi-circular, with the joints alternating north/south and east/west. Here at Lydd my reading was confirmed and the joints obligingly alternated as described.

In the north chapel the 14th century is represented by the effigy of a cross-legged recumbent knight. I think I am correct in saying that the legs of these stone warriors were crossed to signify that the deceased had been a crusader. When one remembers their ferocious conduct on the way to and up and down the Holy Land, or Outremer as they called it, a permanent boast like this makes one realise what utterly different standards of belief and behaviour they had in the Middle Ages. The 17th century, scarcely less violent, is here represented by a tomb chest, around which local elections were held, and by a bust which shelters in a niche in the chancel. Sheltered is the right word, for Thomas Godfrey emerged triumphantly with only superficial damage from the bomb of 1940.

What a super church – and what can have been in the mind of the pilot of that Messerschmitt when he released his bomb?

One of many rural survivors from the past in deepest Kent. What we have here is a tiny farming hamlet and an equally tiny grey flint church that reaches back eight hundred years. It stands on a bank above the road that curves through the village. There is a small nave, a smaller chancel, a north porch confronting the road and a shingled spirelet for the bells at the western end. All is simple and diminutive and follows the plan outline of the earliest stone churches in this country. Compatible with the paired, rectangular construction are the Norman doorways – the northern within the porch and in use, the southern blocked, possibly because it faces the open fields and away from the houses. There are the remains of a small Norman window in the chancel, but this and any others there may once have been are overlaid by matching windows of later styles. The general effect is neat and modest and must have been well suited to the community it served. Now its continued operational existence can only be precarious and it shares the one vicar with two other parishes.

Of course it was firmly locked, although the idea of vandalism in these peaceful and remote surroundings seems absurd. Being so small, the windows were accessible and I could see most of what there is to be seen inside. There is a chunky font – fonts are invariably one of the older, more enduring objects in a church so I daresay that this one is contemporary with the doorways. I could not see any memorials, but there is a handsome Jacobean pulpit, with sounding board above, and a screen (of c.1871 says Pevsner – I did not know that the Victorians installed screens which always seem to me to epitomise the medieval attitude to the separation of clergy and congregation). However, viewed from the outside the most striking feature inside is the decorated chancel ceiling – gold stars and crowns painted on a white ground between the darkened rafters. I am sure it looks stunning from within and must indicate that this church still commands affection and support so perhaps its future is more secure than one might suppose.

The raised churchyard is simply an acre of rough grass from which the headstones have been largely eliminated. The fifty or so of these are ranged against the church, east and west, and elsewhere at the perimeter – to reinforce the fence, it seems. It is a pity; churchyards without their tombstones really do lose their elegiac character. Chillenden's situation above the road minimises the barren aspect and, to this extent, the clearance here is more excusable than is often the case. My sketch was undertaken from the edge of the road below and I could not help feeling encouraged by the friendly waves I received from the occupants of every vehicle which passed my nose. Possibly they thought I was mad, perched on the rim of the highway in mid December.

I hardly expected to find that the village ran to a pub, but there is one, the Griffin's Head, and mentioned by Pevsner to boot. It is a wealden house, another relic from the past, and one in which I was very happy to warm myself after my morning in the open.

KNOWLTON
St. Clement

Knoll farmstead

Like Otterden, Knowlton lies in the shadow of its great house without benefit of any village. It takes persistence to find but it is worth persevering to reach so romantic and private a setting. My preliminary reconnaissance of the small, enclosed churchyard revealed little beyond a two-celled, flint church, securely locked against entry. Baffled but not surprised I began to pace about for an adequate view only to be considerably disconcerted by the arrival of two rangy, proprietorial alsatians and I reached my car only seconds before they did. After a suspicious examination they retired to the churchyard, an eventuality that made me distinctly relieved that I was no longer there. My sketch, probably not from the best angle available, was therefore necessarily conducted with immediate access to the car, a paramount criterion – all things considered I was glad to complete it but reluctant to leave with so little of the church discovered. A church that is virtually an annex to a great house is bound to be of more than usual interest and not to be missed if one can help it.

Fortunately, at this stalemate, two gardeners appeared and they took the alsatians off, three not two it transpired and obedient to their commands the gardeners assured me. Relying on their word, I plucked up sufficient courage to collect the key of the church from the estate office; and very glad I am that I did.

Obviously the little church was built to serve Knowlton Court, its owners and its retainers, with a proper order of precedence being maintained by the family pew on the altar side of the chancel rails. In the unrestored nave, box pews for the staff survive to rest on a black and white tiled floor, overlooked by a three-decked pulpit from which the congregation could be suitably admonished. There are various family memorials on the floor and on the walls but two facing chest tombs in the chancel predominate. The northern is nautical and commemorates Sir John Narborough, admiral of the fleet in the reign of Charles II. Back at home I learnt in my 'Sea Kings of Britain' that Narborough had fought with distinction against the Dutch only to die at sea later of a fever. But not before he had befriended the younger Clowdisley Shovel who, in his turn, rose to be an admiral and, in fact, went on to marry Narborough's widow. Shovel, a tough-looking old sea dog to judge from his portrait, and not the man to be put off by a couple of alsatians, also distinguished himself at sea, chiefly with Rooke in defence of Gibraltar against the French, but he seems to be most remembered today for the stranding of his squadron on the Scilly Isles in 1707. Narborough's two sons were both lost in this disaster, but the sea did not manage to claim Clowdisley; he reached the shore, only to be dispatched by the islanders who were after the ring on his finger. All are commemorated on this one memorial. It would appear from their history that it was only the female members of the family in that generation who lived to enjoy their estate in Kent.

If these remarks seem to concentrate to excess on naval history and guard dogs, I must confess that that is how I shall remember this sequestered place – far from the perils of the sea which it so vividly recalls.

If one approaches Marden from the north west, as I did, one first encounters an industrial estate that looks as if it will transform a wealden village into a modern country town. Perhaps it already has; there is an almost tangible air of prosperity here which is faithfully reflected in the immaculate parish church where all is bright and clean and well-preserved.

The church is surprisingly old when one remembers that the wealden forests must have ruled here once. Nevertheless the Saxons managed a church, probably wooden and now demolished, which was replaced by a dark-brown, sandstone building that ranges from 1190, for the chancel nave and tower base, to 1400, when the French weavers added the north chapel. As a result of two centuries of sporadic building and a 16th century fire, which destroyed the original spire, we now have a church that looks a delightful jumble of styles and materials externally, while internally it might once have been a battleground. I did not know that fire destroys stone, but several of the arcade pillars look as if they have been hit by gunfire.

One approaches the two-storeyed porch along a path paved with ledger stones which, to my mind, make an ideal base for a churchyard path. On the left are the old parish stocks, presented by 'E. Hussey, Lord of the Manor, 1882'. I wonder if he was related to that Hussey who restored so many churches in Kent and rebuilt most of Goodnestone; I expect so. Inside the porch one is briefly disconcerted to be asked by a poster 'Do you have a drink problem?' Fortunately the gorgeous linen-fold door rapidly disperses the memory of such an impertinent question.

Despite the effects of the fire, the interior has been extremely well looked after. There are two organs, mercifully unobtrusive, two pulpits and carpet runners throughout to cover the old stone flags. The font is dated 1662, with an elaborate wooden cover in the shape of a sort of carved tabernacle, to which access is gained by doors; I do not imagine the baby enjoys the experience for it must be even more intimidating than the usual method of baptism. The stained glass windows in the chancel are new, by an associate of Graham Sutherland, whose grave is not too far away at Trottiscliffe. Their design and colouring look to me harsh and violent and not what I would choose for a chancel, but then neither would I choose the Chagall windows at Tudeley. Next to the chancel, the south chapel has recently been partitioned by a carved, painted screen and given smart new pews, both of which in their unfussy, modern design contrast effectively with the fragments of the canopy over the medieval tomb recess in the chapel's south wall.

As with most villages, Marden's church is its jewel and the village has evidently deserved its prize. In the nave, the list of the fallen in the Great War totals seventy and in World War II twenty-four plus four civilians. For a country parish these are higher figures than usual, I suspect. To what extent does an ancient village church like Marden's foster a spirit of patriotism, I wonder; it must have some effect.

There are good parts of Staplehurst and dull parts, mostly the latter, but naturally the church is the focus of the good part at the crest of Staplehurst hill. As befits its commanding position overlooking the Weald towards Cranbrook, this church is old and impressive. In the days when they built churches like this, going to church was more than important, it was obligatory and here at Staplehurst three females went to the stake in the 1550s for refusing to attend the services. What a contradiction between the pitiless sentence and the benevolence of the church today. I would need no more than a whiff of woodsmoke to come to kneel. It does, though, demonstrate how important the church was in the life of the parish and corroborates the magnitude of the effort deployed in their construction and embellishment in those days.

Staplehurst church is celebrated for the ironwork on its unused south door – to enter now one needs to negotiate two doors and a screen at the base of the tower. Quite right too; the south door is far too vulnerable and valuable to be exposed to damage by usage. When one admires this door one is in fact looking at ironwork that dates back to 1050 and is said to depict the Norse Day of Judgment. Fishes and sea monsters, beautifully wrought, swarm on the upper half of the door and there cannot be much doubt that the smith who made it had Viking blood in his veins. The iron strapwork reeks of the Icelandic sagas and pagan superstition. It is an experience simply to contemplate it in its disused porch.

Almost as evocative as the hinges are the traces of an anchorite's cell on the north side of the chancel. All that remains now is a 6 x 4 foot depression in the ground, roughly paved by stone flags. Here the would-be saint was immured, to be fed and watered through a hole in the chancel wall. How he managed the other problems of life I cannot imagine, but he must have had his methods; probably he did not last long in his tomb.

A contemporary of the martyred females, Walter Mayney, being a Sheriff of Kent, suffered rather less and was buried beneath the south chapel, to be commemorated by a substantial chest-tomb. The chest-tomb remains but of the brass, only that of his second wife has been left. Other prominent parishioners had their coats of arms inserted in stained glass in the windows along the north side of the nave. They are joined by the arms of Kent, St. John's College, Cambridge, Canterbury and the 'Pelican in her Piety', the symbolism of which I ought to know but do not.

They were wise to choose the north wall for the pillars between the nave and the south aisle lean alarmingly downhill. The pamphlet suggests that these pillars, standing on the foundations of the removed south wall, lean deliberately, presumably to accommodate the displaced roof. That makes the stability of the church even more suspect, but this part of the church dates from the 12th and 13th centuries so one should not exaggerate the danger. Probably the outside wall and the porch that houses the Viking doorway keep the whole edifice upright. For peace of mind it is as well to examine the doorway before encountering the pillars.

What a stimulating church with which to start 1986.

Closely cordoned by studded cottages and churchyard trees, Smarden church is not an easy subject to draw. Though full of promise, each view must make a compromise with obstruction. In the end I settled for a perch in the picturesque northeast entrance under the overhang of one cottage and alongside Parsonage House. Both cottages are now antique shops which will give a clue to the character of this period hamlet. On the cottage wall to my left were five shields awarded to Smarden as 'Best Kept Village' and looking round it is not difficult to see why Smarden must always be a hot favourite for this worthy competition. Immediately in front of me on the ground lay a stone dated 1705, inscribed as 'last resting place of . . . ' – surely not where it now rests – and on the grass nearby eight muscovy ducks grazed, unconcerned by my presence. Sheep are often seen in a churchyard; muscovy ducks are a first for me, but I imagine they belonged to one of the cottagers, no doubt exercising some ancient right of pannage or its avian equivalent.

Smarden church is a 14th century ragstone structure of nave and chancel, but something obviously existed here before the present building as the list of vicars goes back to 1205. The tower, of Bethersden marble, is later by a century, which takes it into the Perpendicular period. There is the regulation stair turret to add distinction to it but not, alas, to my sketch. The church is noted for its extra wide nave with no arcade pillars to help take some of the thrust of the roof. Instead the rafters are held rigidly together by scissors of auxiliary rafters; an arrangement which provides an interesting roof, but creates a rather hangar-like impression in the nave. Nevertheless, it also leaves one with a healthy respect for the mathematical capacity of whoever worked out, way back in the 1300s, the stresses and strains involved in spanning 36 feet in one go.

The chancel walls have been cleaned of all plaster to reveal the rough texture of the rubble ragstone – it may seem at variance with the nave, but certainly it is in keeping with the piscinas, the wafer oven, the arched recesses and the low south window, all of which bear the look of great age, unchanged after centuries of disuse. One of the piscinas contains two small shelves, 'credences' the pamphlet says. It goes on to say that poisoning in church was not unknown in the Middle Ages and that tasters were employed, their test sample being placed on the credence shelf. I am not sure I find this hypothesis entirely credible.

There are two side chapels, or at least relics of them. Both are defined by a double row of arches framing a wall-painted surface. The south chapel exhibits an altar stone embedded in the wall and in the north chapel one encounters a hostile-looking marble head which glares down from a window splay. Its purpose or message is not known to the authorities at the church today. My understanding is that grotesque heads, like this one, were generally designed to scare away devils; if that supposition is accepted, one might expect the head to face outwards, not down on the congregation, unless the latter was reckoned to be sinful. An angel once again shares this window, more encouraging for today's equally sinful parishioners, I have no doubt.

An old-fashioned village on the road to Sandwich with its best parts at the crown of the hill where the church is. If ever anywhere needs a by-pass, it must be Ash. The houses and churchyard crowd the through road and both are menaced and contaminated by the container lorries. Perhaps the Channel tunnel will bring relief.

Originally part of the royal manor of Wingham, Ash was detached and given by Athelstan, the Saxon king, to the See of Canterbury which after all those years is still patron of the living. One can understand, therefore, why a relatively grand church has ensued in a strip of countryside that only seems remarkable today for its beauty. The church is cruciform, and that rare treat, sketchable from any angle. With the tower in the centre of the building, distorted vertical perspective is not a problem, or at least not so much of a problem as it often is. My view was dictated by the weather; I needed a cottage at my back between me and the wind and the rain. And I could not help but be attracted, for my foreground, by those ancient, ornamental rococo headstones which line the path. Of the part of church that confronted me, the west end of the north aisle is said to be the oldest, dating from circa 1150 when it formed the base of a vanished Norman tower. With that in mind I examined the flints to the best of my ability, but they did not say 'tower' to me; nor could I identify with confidence the reputed sill of the arrowslit under the eaves. Certainly the tracery of the west window, post Norman, is tortuous and difficult and I was grateful for the helpful presence of the intervening tombstones.

Distinguished as the exterior of this Early English church and its elegiac church-yard are, the interior must call for most attention. The pamphlet claims that Ash has the best inventory of monumental effigies in the county; I would not dream of disputing that boast for there are no less than three armour-clad knights and two of their ladies. One pair lies on a chest-tomb, the others separately in 'windows' in the wall between the chancel and the north chapel. These recumbent, life-size figures were painted once, but now they look worn and dusty. Since they are secure from the weather, one wonders how such stone figures became so mutilated and eroded, but I suppose much that is unexpected can happen in the course of five hundred years. There are, as well, brasses in profusion on the floors. One represents the daughter of Sir John Oldcastle, the Falstaff of Shakespeare's plays, who came to an untimely end through his lollardry. The Lollards were liberal with their criticisms of the ecclesiastical abuses of their day so I suppose that Maud Clitherow, née Old-castle, can be counted lucky to have her place on the floor under the central tower.

Aside from the outstanding collection of monuments, the most striking features of the interior are the four massive 16th century columns that support the Perpen-dicular tower. They seem to reach to the sky in a combination of grace and strength. Naturally their masons would have been proud of and delighted with their achieve-ment and they are said to have left their marks on one of the pillars. As someone who once laid a brick wall all of five feet high, I should like to have paid my respects but try as I might, I could find no trace of their marks. My wall is signed too.

WOODNESBOROUGH
St. Mary the Virgin

It is an irony that the churches I most prefer, those that are isolated and inconspicuous, insignificant in terms of worldly consequence, are those that are invariably locked so that one is denied the extra pleasure of pottering about inside a rural museum piece undisturbed by manifestations of 20th century progress.

At first sight Woodnesborough church seemed such an example although, exposed as it is on the top of its windswept hill, it can hardly be described as inconspicuous. Neither can the hill be said to have been insignificant in the past. Tradition has it that the hill was sacred to pagan Britons, hence the name, and that one of their kings, Vortimer, wished to be buried here so that his bones might threaten and discourage Saxon invaders from coming ashore at Richborough. His followers failed to carry out his wishes when he died in 457 and the landings continued to such an extent that, as my history book records, the conquest of Kent by the Jutes was complete by 494. From the churchyard one can see far into Pegwell Bay where St. Augustine, also undeterred by Vortimer, landed in 597, left the imprint of his foot (sandal surely) in the rock, if one can believe the legend, and substituted Christianity for paganism.

The church, like its village, is modest; flint walls enclose a nave and two aisles — a description which reads more impressively than the dimensions allow. What does appeal here, visually, and makes Woodnesborough so signal a find is the tower with its wooden balustrade of turned balusters surrounding the lead-covered Georgian cupola. A bit more curvature and the latter could have been an onion top. I have drawn cupolas on towers in Kent before, but none that I can remember having an elegant wooden balustrade.

True to theory, the church was locked and its windows are so placed and glazed that nothing of the interior could be made out. Pevsner tells us that the church originated before 1200 so it is genuinely venerable even if restoration gives it a more recent appearance. Its early origin explains the existence of vaulted sedilia which so aroused the admiration of Messrs. Boorman and Torr that they awarded this feature of Woodnesborough church a whole page of description and illustration in their excellent and informed book on Kent's churches. They even go so far as to allot five other references to the church, which serves to contradict my first impression of an obscure building of no great consequence. I can now understand, if not exactly condone, the locked door at Woodnesborough when no-one is about. This church is a museum piece.

From where I sat to make my sketch, I could not help reflecting on the human vanity that inspires such self-important memorials as those that occupy my foreground and on the extent to which time and weather frustrate hopes of monumental immortality. The inscriptions are largely obliterated and those they commemorate doubtless forgotten. At least they have escaped the more undignified fate of many of the headstones; moved to the south wall of the churchyard, these stones lie flat on the ground — soon to be buried by creeper and weed and, like the pagan superstitions before them, finally to be absorbed by the myths of Woden's hill.

SANDHURST
St. Nicholas

Sandy wood

I was delighted with Sandhurst and myself when together we broke the unrelenting siege of Siberian weather that was February 1986. It had been a most frustrating month, agonisingly cold and bitter, but Monday 3rd March promised better things – relief from the east wind, sunshine and a temperature just above zero. The weather, in fact, did not quite live up to its promise, but the church did and I felt rejuvenated even if it entailed sitting on a carpet of snow.

The church stands well away from its village, on a hill overlooking the Rother where it marks the boundary between Kent and Sussex as it slides down to Rye and the sea. From here one can see Bodiam castle which is sited, the pamphlet says, so as to be visible from the watch-tower church. That may account for Bodiam being where it is but not for the church, two miles from its village astride the Roman road from Hastings to Rochester. There is supposed, apparently without foundation, to have been a plague pit in the churchyard and that might be a reason for the separation of village and church. At all events I am sure the church is better off in semi-isolation on its hill, although presumably the vicar would not agree.

The most striking feature of this honey-coloured building, both externally and internally, is the 15th century tower. It dominates the rest of the church and the landscape. Rectangular and formed of squared blocks, set more or less in regular courses, it is topped by a band of brickwork; Pevsner suggests that the tower has lost its conventional top which may explain the bricks. I was intrigued to see several instances of clay tiles, laid flat, between the stones. However enjoyable visually, this practice always surprises me. I cannot imagine the mason who was responsible for the construction of this massive tower ever allowing his stonework to be adulterated by soft clay tiles; perhaps they are make and mend after his time, but surely one does not bolster stone with clay. Internally the tower stands on elaborate compound piers which create five arches at the base. Magnificent it looks and well suited to house on the floor the bell, John, which is its contemporary, and the font which is even older. Much of the church is later and restored and does not really compare. There are two aisles, octagonal arcade pillars and Early English clerestory windows which, the guide suggests, derive from an earlier building here (one can understand foundations being pressed into the service of a replacement, but the salvage of windows from high up in the roof for re-use is less easy to comprehend). One of the few memorials is an aisle window engraved in memory of a recent vicar – definitely preferable to stained glass, I thought – and I was particularly reassured to notice it included my view of the church as also did at least one of the hassocks. Very likely my sketch is the obvious angle to choose, but I was influenced as much by the depth of wind-blown snow as by anything.

Despite the scarcity of monuments to past celebrities or local worthies, Sandhurst has had its own brief brush with history. Apparently Titus Oates was assistant curate here in the 17th century. How strange, inappropriate even, that an innocent curacy in this dignified, sentinel church at the back of beyond should develop into a conspiratorial career that ended eventually with the pillory and imprisonment.

EASTRY
St. Mary the Virgin

There are a great many churches in this rather empty quarter of east Kent inland from Deal, and it is said that from the top of Eastry's tower one can see seventeen of them. If one wanted a vantage from which to make the count, there could not be a more satisfactory observation point than here, combining height with enrichment externally and age with strength. Like all good Norman towers there is something very uncompromising about Eastry's and, although it is made of flint, any weakness in the building material is more than made up by the generous dimensions of the walls. It has stood since the 12th century and it was presumably within its shelter that Archbishop Becket hid when seeking refuge from Henry II after his quarrel in 1164 about who could try the clergy, king or cloth. In the light of history it seems clear that both have lost to the People. The tower forms the focus of my sketch, as it must of any picture of this church, and after its splendour the nave and chancel seem rather commonplace from the outside.

The doors were locked, surprisingly, when one remembers that Eastry is quite a big, and no doubt law-abiding, village and the church is comfortably tucked away down a side street that leads to the equally, or even more, historic Eastry Court. One enters, when one can, through a characteristic Norman west door which today is obscured by a curious, unattractive lateral porch. Fortunately for me I was saved a trek to the vicarage for the key by the fortuitous arrival of one of the flower arrangers and I gratefully followed her in. The interior, which is essentially of the next period, Early English, is spacious and dignified with the walls much embellished by hanging memorials of what one might describe as the relief — obelisk type. The most prominent of these is that to a naval captain, native of Eastry, who died of wounds received at the battle of the Glorious First of June in 1794 when the English under the seventy-year old Lord Howe defeated the French revolutionary fleet off Ushant. It is extraordinary how vividly these old village churches bring alive the long history of this country and it is one of their fascinations for me. Indeed, any church that lacks memorials is diminished, I think, and I am sure that future generations will regret today's secularisation that discourages immortalisation in stone. Eastry does not suffer in this way for it was not only Captain Harvey RN but also Thomas Becket, Archbishop, who sent me to the history book.

Circular pillars support the arcades that divide the nave from the aisles. All, that is, except one, which is octagonal, and it was on this singular individual that I found the famous incised diagram, said to represent a perpetual calendar — the vicar's version of the Nautical Almanac — from which the dates of feast days may be calculated. It seemed incomprehensible, as did the Almanac in my naval days, and one wonders how often it contradicted the edicts of Rome or Canterbury or Whitby. Another relic from the medieval past is a series of wall paintings in medallion form above the chancel arch. Faded, like the calendar, these paintings are a rarity but inscrutable. Together with the distinguished Norman tower and the historical associations, these artefacts make Eastry the star amongst the seventeen satellites that can be seen on a clear day.

No more than a mile from the confident bulk of Eastry, little Ham church, without a village to its name, is not easy to find. What was it ever doing here with only Ham manor for company and with Eastry perfectly capable of meeting the religious needs of the scattered population for miles around? There is no clue from its situation today (March 1986). According to Pevsner's 1976 edition of the Kent buildings, I could expect to find a neat Early English church of tiny nave and chancel. What in fact I found appeared at first glance to be a neat Victorian church of miniature dimensions in a scene of rural desolation. The manor farm, which intruded without hindrance on to the defenceless churchyard, sprawled untidily alongside and lent none of that atmosphere of comfortable harmony that farms by churches generally do. The churchyard seemed forlorn; tombstones discarded and displaced, some stacked in a decrepit, spidery hut at the west end of the church, others disturbed by saplings which are well on the way to reverting the churchyard to scrub. The lych-gate, pleasant enough, stands isolated with no fence or wall or hedge to link it with its churchyard and I parked my car on what I assumed to be hard-standing between it and the chancel. Such surroundings did not promise well for the church.

The knapped-flint walls looked to be in pretty good condition – the restoration in 1880 being responsible no doubt – and that is what conveyed the fleeting Victorian impression. The south porch, though, gave the first discouraging intimation. With inner and outer doors padlocked, all the porch contained was what I took to be a cement mixer; not an encouraging implement to find in a church unless repairs are in progress, which a hundred years after the Victorian rescue, they clearly were not. A broken pane in one of the windows revealed a sunken interior, several feet below ground level, in which no trace of ecclesiastical purpose or furnishing remained. Instead of rows of pews there was an unseemly jumble of miscellaneous litter and the nave seemed to have degenerated into a temporary workshop and haphazard store. Similarly the chancel had become secularised and debased.

When I had finished my rough sketch, which, surprisingly considering the state of the church and churchyard, turned out rather well pictorially speaking, I found in the lych-gate what I had subconsciously been looking for. Here, fastened to the timbers, was a notice saying that the church had become a private residence (sic) and a stained-glass studio and that, if anyone wished to visit or tend the grave stones forming the churchyard, they should apply in writing to an address in Sandwich. By the look of things, few have. When Charles Igglesden came here in 1926 to describe the church he reported it to be 'well groomed inside and out'. I wonder what he would report today or, indeed, what Jane Woodruff, who was buried in 1775 and lies with her husband beside the misused porch, would make of it all: consternation at the very least.

ALKHAM
St. Anthony the Martyr

Heathen temple settlement

Alkham is a deceptive village and it is possible to drive through it without sighting the church, as I did. There is a pervading feeling of the urban presence of Folkestone and Dover which bracket the village on either side and on a misty day the harbour foghorns of these ports echo persistently across Alkham valley. The church, happily on its slope above the through road and behind the pub, seems immune from civic progress and one hopes that it will remain that way.

The people here have in fact possessed a church from at least the time of the Conquest, but the present flint structure dates from the 13th century and is largely Early English. The first recorded rector, Herbert, son of the Lord of the Barony of Folkestone, had the living from 1199-1203, so he must have officiated in the smaller Norman church of which the only surviving traces are to be found embedded in the walls; I thought I recognised evidence of this in the south-east corner of the chancel, but no doubt an expert could correct me. To revert to Herbert, one can read all about him and his successors in one of the splendidly informative listings prepared by the Reverend Mr Frampton. He provides a church history plus potted biographies of the incumbents. I wish, however, that Mr Frampton's type face was not so small – one suspects that it is mostly the elderly who will read these accounts and, in the uncertain week-day light of a church, that is not so easily done, but well worth the effort.

Herbert lies below a great engraved stone coffin slab on the floor of the north chapel beside the blind shafted arcading that is responsible for the acclaim accorded to this church. As well as Herbert's slab, there is a fine assembly of grey-black ledger stones, mostly to members of the same family, on the chancel floor, but these, of course, are about five hundred years more recent than that of the first rector.

The main impression one gains externally is that of an ancient flint-dark church, backed by tall trees, above its gentle valley. It is a building of sufficient size to justify a gallery of circular clerestory windows. Once indeed it was larger than it is today; blanked arches in the north wall of the nave suggest a north aisle which would certainly have accommodated the chapel more coherently in the overall plan. One wonders why it was demolished. One of the vicars, it is chronicled, refused to unlock the church for 'the space of 12 to 13 weeks in 1592'; he probably had other parishes to attend to but the alleged lockout does suggest a lack of enthusiasm for Alkham and might that not convey an easy acceptance of the necessity for reduction? Frampton's record has the answer, I expect.

My drawing here includes the faint outline of the arcade that once opened on to the demolished aisle, the squat west tower and the corner of the obtruding north chapel wherein lies the founding father. It is the shadowed, unfrequented side. I had hoped to make a more withdrawn sketch from the paddock of the old rectory beyond the churchyard wall, but two inquisitive and persevering donkeys prevented me. They seemed to expect a goody and even when I had retreated to the churchyard their gusty breath disturbed the hairs on the back of my neck. At least they were friendly.

220

Lydden may not be a church that figures in many of the listings of the more fashionable churches in Kent, but I found it quite charming and I am surprised that Arthur Mee overlooked it. It is totally unassuming, of great antiquity and authenticity, and a church that any parish should and would, and no doubt Lydden does, cherish. It may make no proud claim to architectural significance or religious experience, but it is exactly the sort of church that, in its unpretentious way, epitomises the stability and identity of the English countryside. So I found it much more of a pleasure than I could have reasonably expected.

The church occupies the north slope of a shallow valley which it shares with a farmstead that is evidently undergoing an energetic rescue from past neglect. The farmhouse is where the key is kept; I am always astonished by the grace with which the key is surrendered by the custodians and I would like, before I forget and with respect to Lydden, to pay a sort of 'compliment incognito' to all those voluntary caretakers of lonely churches. I could wish, but with little confidence, that I would be half as benevolent in their place.

The church has not been neglected so far as one can tell. It is sturdy and simple with walls that are three feet thick; 13th century says Pevsner, 11th century in origin says the church, and doubtless both are right. There is a small nave which runs on into the chancel, a west tower, supported by but one buttress on the downhill side, and a south porch. For some reason all the apertures on the west side of the tower have been blocked, leaving virtually no provision for the sound of the bells to carry, which is odd when one remembers that the hamlet is dispersed away down the valley and probably at the limit of earshot. The porch is very old and distinctly primitive, of painted but unplastered flints. Within, the equally old doorway is a puzzle; its arch is somewhat pointed whereas its door is ogee shaped. The two do not match and clearly were never made for each other. I was even more careful than usual to make sure that this anomaly did not swing to and lock behind me when I entered.

Despite its patent simplicity externally, the interior is distinguished by two elaborate carved recesses in the south wall of the nave. One of these, designed for the local land-holding family in the Middle Ages, bears their armorial shields on the base in place of the usual recumbent effigy which at least generalises the memorial rather than concentrating on the individual. These two tomb niches take up most of the space between the south doorway and the chancel arch and seem almost to be the raison d'être for the church. Above them, facing east where the nave abuts on the chancel, there glows a tiny Norman window which, in 1952, was given a stained glass light – a successful marriage of the 12th and 20th centuries, it seemed.

I have adopted the north side again for my sketch, mainly because the background from this viewpoint seemed an improvement on the modern houses in the other direction. The fact of the matter is, when a church is eight hundred years old, one is asking for the impossible to expect a contemporary background. Only the churchyard yews will genuinely qualify.

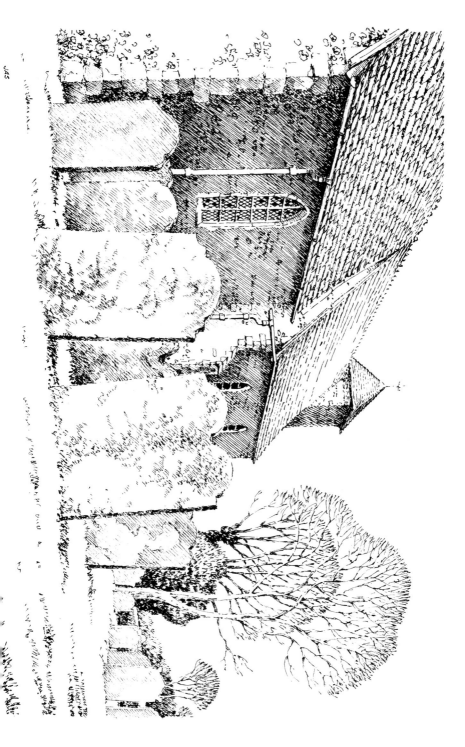

EYTHORNE
St. Peter and St. Paul

An Early English church in a Kent mining village which, notwithstanding the troubles of the coal industry in 1984/5, maintains at least one well-frequented and cheerful pub where, incidentally and perhaps consequentially, the prices were noticeably lower than those of many traditional country pubs. The small flint church does look rather out of place, but of course it was here long before the adjacent colliery of Tilmanstone or before the now defunct mineral railway from Shepherds-well to Eastry was driven through the village. One might more appropriately say that the village looks out of place.

The church consists of a modest south nave and chancel, a lesser north aisle and chapel, and a north west tower. The small, inconspicuous, west door to the nave has now been superseded by the more commodious brick-vaulted chamber at the base of the tower through which one enters the body of the church. The tower, being a later addition, as the blocked doorway testifies, is Perpendicular – but only just, I would surmise. A few feet below the parapet it has been necessary to bind the whole structure together with an iron strap and crossed iron stanchions – these braces being backed up by brick at the quoins; still, despite such signs of collapse averted, the tower looks good and solid and should outlast the looming winding gear a mile to the north.

Once inside, the broad, rectangular piers of the arcade between nave and aisle remind one of the fact that this church dates from about 1200. Then there was probably a screen between nave and chancel; today a beam across the chancel arch carries a central crucifix and two flanking statues to convey something of the religious atmosphere of the past before the Reformation. The floor is paved with a group of six or seven magnificent ledger stones spanning the years between 1661 and 1765; it is a pity that such memorials are no longer the fashion – they do as much for the flooring of a church as a few Persian rugs do for a house. Contemporary with the ledger stones is a rescued lead font, the side panels of which share representation of naked females with the date, 1628; primly the font is so arranged to display the date and hide the ladies. Less historic and less erotic is a careful model of the church made from 13,174 matchsticks – a case of love, perseverance and arithmetic. Even more up to date is the new organ, a pretty little instrument which in 1979 replaced a monstrosity, the vicar said, that previously monopolised the north chapel.

This is a very attractive little church, inside and out. There are many like it in Kent and there is nothing particularly remarkable about this one, except perhaps in the contrast between its mellow flint walls and the surrounding modern village. It is well looked after; the church inside was spotless and the rambling churchyard outside as neat and tidy as could be expected bearing in mind the capacity of nature to revert to the jungle in a year or two of neglect. There is no sign of that here.

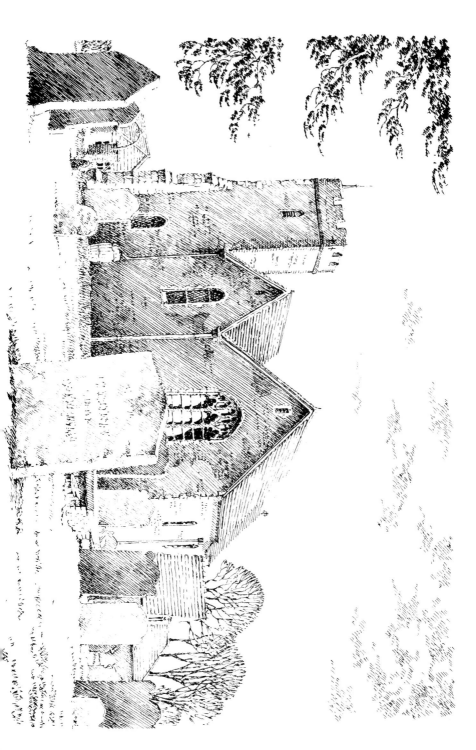

Waldershare is the sort of country church that has had its day and must inevitably retreat into oblivion. All the visible evidence supports this conclusion and a dusty notice in the porch to the effect that the church was declared redundant in 1982 and leased to the 'All Saints Waldershare Trust' confirms the end of its active life.

It lies some way back from the Sandwich to Dover road, down an inconspicuous track that claims to be part of the North Downs Way. There is a house adjoining and a pub on the main road, but otherwise nothing except scrub and the sweeping emptiness of Waldershare Park. It is the church of the Park without a doubt, but why so remote from the great house? With no parish or congregation or purpose, it must decline into the shadows of the future, a shrine to past owners of the Park and a rendezvous for ramblers. There was a Norman church here for the first Norman landholder; little good it did him for he was soundly cursed by a Saxon girl and suffered accordingly. Successive owners of the Park thereafter seem to have developed the church as their mausoleum by adding south and north chapels to the central chancel. First came the Berties and then a Sandwich tradesman who made good in the City, sufficiently good in fact to build himself a Queen Anne mansion in the Park. The church was locked but, by hoisting myself up on the window sills, I could just briefly make out the contents of the two chapels. In the north, entirely filling the space, is the sculpted, figured column to Sir Henry Furnese, the City sheriff, late of Sandwich. Opposite, in the south, lying hand in hand on a massive chest-tomb, are the Berties. It is difficult to describe one's sensations when contemplating the Berties, locked and petrified in their darkened chamber, season after season and year after year. It seemed somehow sad, even morbid, and yet not so; in a minor way it is Kent's version of a pharaoh's tomb. I was very glad to have glimpsed these imprisoned memorials even if only by extreme muscular exertion of the cat burglar variety.

The rest of the church did not seem interesting externally; the nave was restored in 1886 but, a mere hundred years later, the bellcote has come to grief and the bell to the ground beside the porch. The chancel, to judge from a photograph, was fairly thoroughly done up by the Victorians, but its decorations must now fade unseen. When these great memorials and the restoration were commissioned, did the sponsors ever envisage solitary redundancy – and would they have persisted if they did, I wonder? One would like to think so.

The churchyard, obviously under attack today from encroaching saplings, is wild and romantic. In a far corner lies the vault of the Guilfords, more recent owners of the Park. Here in an enclosure, roughly the size of a squash court, the sixth, seventh and eighth earls of Guilford and their respective families, sixteen all told, rest commemorated in the open. There is space for a further nineteen and nothing could be better, I think, than to join one's forebears under the ageing, sweeping yews, safe in this hidden churchyard from the despoliation of the modern world outside.

One finds this church in a valley, a mile down a winding lane from the present-day village of Challock Lees. It is an idyllic setting; a single farmstead, fields and woods, and nothing else but a few unconcerned pheasants in the stubble. Once the turnpike ran past the church and the village lay around. Then in 1589 the land was enclosed within Eastwell Park, the road was diverted and the by-passed village withered so that no trace at all remains today. The enclosure must have seemed ruthless at the time, but it has left us with an enchanting little church in solitary state amongst the woods.

When I arrived to sketch it knowing its isolated situation, I was surprised to find three young girls seated by the porch devouring a premature picnic lunch on the first day of their Easter holiday. The church was locked because, said one of the trio, the church had been robbed and, amongst other things, the bishop's chair taken. Fortunately her father is a professional wood carver and he had made the replacement chair, she stated with justifiable pride. I could see it clearly through the low windows; indeed the locked door was no bar to an inspection of the interior, the windows being accessible and blessed with transparent glass.

The church is noteworthy for recent restoration. There was bomb damage in the 1939-45 war and the nave roof collapsed shortly afterwards necessitating drastic remedial action so that now we have an exceedingly remote little church in apple-pie order; of museum quality almost. There are three screens – Perpendicular for the chapel and tower, Victorian (and late of the ruined Eastwell church) for the chancel. The murals in the chancel and chapel are not to be missed – from time to time one sees the faded colours of medieval wall painting, but never before, in my admittedly limited experience, the 20th century version. The 20th century is not disgraced here. The work in the chapel is that of two students of the Royal Academy School and that in the chancel the contribution of an actual Royal Academician, so demonstrably the paintings are of the highest quality. One hopes they will survive the centuries as well as, or better than, their medieval predecessors; I have every hope though that the work will have been recorded on film and thus rendered relatively imperishable.

The external fabric of this church is 13th century with a 14th century tower; constructed of flint with ironstone blocks here and there like currants in a bun. There has been redesign, not simply reconstruction, as the voussoir stones above the west window testify. Similarly there is the shadow of a north porch above the disused north door. Unchanged from the past are two anamalistic gargoyles at the west end of the narrow south aisle and male and female heads as label stops to a south window. The female head, notwithstanding the period headdress, is nondescript; the male is a medieval version of Charles Laughton to the life. Just as the actor was autocratic in his roles, so the stone head leers down with none of the humility proper to a churchgoer of the Middle Ages.

CHARTHAM
St. Mary

Chartham village does not live up to its church. Although there is a pleasant open green to the west of the churchyard wall the coming of the railway brought in its train progress in the shape of light industry. Today, in terms of visual impact, the impressive 13th century church is outgunned by the range of buildings of the Wiggins Teape paper factory. Fortunately for me they keep the key of the church there and I was able to collect it from the amiable gatekeeper without too much difficulty.

Externally, the knapped-flint walls of the church present a somewhat severe and ordered face to the world. It is cruciform in shape and the windows, complete with split cusps, are well above ground level and beyond the reach of prying eyes. So it was as well for me that I could unlock the porch doors. Equally so for the quartet of twelve-year old scouts who had come from Burham, near Rochester along the Pilgrims' Way and were now approaching journey's end. They were without a care and, I am sure, enjoying themselves enormously.

The magnet that draws visitors to Chartham (although I should add that on Maundy Thursday my only companions were the scouts) must be the brass memorial to Sir Robert de Septvans. This brass, the oldest in Kent and fourth oldest in England, is life size and shows the knight, bare headed and in full military order, at the height of his powers, not in old age. His hands are clasped in prayer and his expression is composed and benign; he looks peaceful and the massive sword more a weapon for the defence of the innocent than for the slaughter of the infidel. He is superb, no better word for it, and certainly the sort to have on one's side. His heraldic device is a winnowing fan; there are seven of these shapeless sou'westers inscribed on his surcoat and they are said to be a pun on his name. I rather wonder, though, which came first, the fans or the name.

I was thrilled to find this celebrated brass; it is the largest and clearest that I have ever seen, complete in every detail except for a small segment of the left foot. But if I had not already known of its existence in Chartham church I should never have seen it. It lies, hidden behind a curtain and protected by a dingy strip of carpet, on the floor of the north transept which it shares unceremoniously with the organ and a litter of lumber. Originally it lay in the centre of the chancel and was, I presume, moved to its present site at the time of the Victorian restoration of the sanctuary. One cannot object to that, but one can reasonably criticise Sir Robert's present treatment in the north transept. Preservation is the standard excuse for the carpet cover, but that does not acquit the pile of lumber alongside. For something as ancient and honourable as this brass, display is proper, not concealment. No-one is going to steal the brass, which it is not, but we all want to admire it — it is good for us and fosters our sense of inheritance.

NONINGTON   *Nunna's farmstead*
St. Mary

Nonington village must by now, because of the proximity of Snowdown colliery, have become a combination of mining village and farming community. The pub where I had beer and sandwiches, with its small billiard table, seemed to reflect the former while the church, safely tucked away at the end of Vicarage Lane, continues to project the rural past. I called in at the colliery on my way to Nonington to inquire why the Kent coalfields seem to dispense with slag heaps. The only person I found in the apparently, but not I was informed in practice, moribund colliery said that there were slag heaps all right in Kent but that they kept them out of sight. Clever old Kent and well done the Coal Board.

The church is very neat and trim; Early English, of flint with most carefully bricked and drained footings to the walls. Perhaps the miners' awareness of the dangers of subsidence has affected the care of the church — for the good naturally. The windows are rather few, mostly restored and fitted with impenetrable glass. This was a pity as the church was locked and the vicarage, from whence the key could be obtained, empty. Observing that Nonington is the seat of the vicar of Chillenden, Goodnestone and Womenswold as well, all equally deserving churches, and parishes too no doubt, the absence of anyone at the vicarage was not surprising. But it did mean that the interior here remained an unopened oyster so far as I was concerned. There have been generations of landed families hereabouts in the past and one might have expected to find an effigy or ledger stone or family in relief to remind one of vanished glories, but the omniscient Pevsner is silent. So one may conclude, with a degree of confidence I think, that it is the fabric here and not the contents that attracts.

Perforce I was content with the exterior. The church stands in a pleasant little churchyard, well stocked with headstones and most still in situ, even if some do seem to have been used to reinforce the crumbled brick and flint churchyard wall. Although I believe the lancet windows at the east end of the church merit most consideration, I found the simple tower at the north west corner the most memorable feature. It is flint, like the rest of the church, but almost entirely without ornament and with the minimum of apertures, and no door. One surprise they have here is the memorial to the fallen of the 1914-18 war which has been incorporated in the Victorian buttress at the south west corner of the nave. It seems an extremely good idea and I wonder why it is not more copied.

As with most church restorations, the south facade, where the porch is, has had the attention, down to the dated rain water hods, while the north has been allowed to mellow undisturbed. It was too cold and sunless to sketch from there on my visit but, in compensation, my perch on the edge of the wealden farmhouse garden was shared, for a brief while, with a quartet of ornamental birds of the peacock variety — a rare treat and a vast improvement on dogs.

TILMANSTONE
St. Andrew

Tilman's farmstead

There may be a colliery called Tilmanstone not far away, at Eythorne to be precise, but Tilmanstone church and village are light years away from the NCB and the NUM. This is a typical hamlet, prudently set back from the main road, with the ancient church high on a bank above the lane as it winds through the scattering of village houses. In fact my view necessitated a perilous balancing act at the edge of the churchyard with no more than a sapling between me and the hard road ten feet below. It was a slightly precarious situation even if the outcome was worth the unease.

The church was well worth the risk. Certainly not a 'small mean building' as was observed in 1790. Quite the reverse; a tranquil survivor from the past that fully deserves the attention it obviously enjoys today. The south doorway in its mini-porch is Norman with the characteristic semi-circular tympanum above the lintel to prove it. There are small Norman windows in the nave walls, but tower and chancel are later, although not by much. There is an enormous old yew to the west which, in this locality, seemed almost as old as the coal measures successfully predicted by Mr Godwin-Austen to lie below the unsuspecting fields of Kent. To be less extravagant, Arthur Mee wrote that the yew must be at least seven hundred years old and I wish I had had the presence of mind, when I had the opportunity, to take a live sprig for potting on at home.

The church door was locked but the key, not far away, was surrendered without hesitation and with the customary goodwill to a total stranger of dishevelled appearance.

It was delightful inside, past the Maltese cross beside the jamb of the doorway, just a small nave and smaller chancel – grey plastered walls cosily enclosing the limited space for a sparse congregation, with a Victorian screen to distance the priest from the people. The church makes much of the 16th century brass in the chancel wall but more exceptional, in a country church at least, are the framed fragments of velvet tapestry. One, a cushion cover, was referred to London for authentication; its pattern of Moorish arabesques resembled that of a footstool beneath the feet of Henry VIII in a portrait by Holbein. Experts identified the piece as 16th century but did not, I read, commit themselves to a royal provenance.

Another rarity possessed by Tilmanstone is a plan, held by the churchwarden, of the locality and identity of the graves in the churchyard. Such a record, uncommon and interesting in itself, must also, I would think, serve to discourage the misguided eviction of headstones from their rightful places to the perimeter or worse. Two final idiosyncrasies that distinguish this church from many others are, first, a metal weather vane in the shape of a bird, a swan possibly, with widespread wings and outstretched neck and second, beside the lych-gate, punishment stocks designed for two. If the instrument could be brought back within the law and operated by the churchwarden as necessary, there might be less need to lock this church – or any other!

JAS

One sees the winding gear of Betteshanger colliery on the horizon long before the church comes into view. Still, once in the church, past the prominent bale vault by the crumbling wall, all such 20th century intrusions are happily forgotten and one is more or less catapulted back into the 12th century in an 18th century frame. Earlier even — for this cruciform Norman church is the successor of a church built less than fifty years after St. Augustine landed six miles away at Ebbsfleet. They say that Saxon material was economically incorporated in the Norman fabric and I wish I had managed to identify something contemporary with the foundation of Christendom in this country.

The overriding impression that one derives from Northbourne church is one of strength and resistance to attack or change. Perhaps this is a characteristic of cruciform churches. There are very few in Kent and two others that come to mind, Boughton Monchelsea and Boughton Aluph, both exhibit this solid, permanent quality; all three are a pleasure to see and a treasure to be preserved. The tower, intended here for defensive purposes against attack by the Danes and later the French, once had an external staircase one step of which remains to protrude from the north transept. In contrast to the collapse of industry at Betteshanger colliery, Northbourne conveys no symptoms of decay or neglect and, situated where it is in rural Kent, there is little danger of change.

Appropriately one steps down into the church through a typical Norman doorway; the nave is narrow and lofty but its stark simplicity is more than redeemed by the four Norman arches which form the crossing below the square, squat tower. It is, however, the south transept, which is the province of the Sandys family, that rivets the attention at Northbourne. Their vault is here, but what dominates is the hanging memorial to Sir Edwin Sandys (1561-1629) and his wife. There are no other comparable monuments to the family so one imagines that later generations were content for their achievements to be publicly stated by this one display. The carving is elaborate and elegant and the whole is sumptuous and ostentatious with Sir Edwin's claim on history inscribed in Latin on the obituary panel above his reclining figure. For the benefit of the majority like myself, who cannot now translate beyond 'hic jacet', three hundred years after the founding of Virginia the American and British Commonwealth Association of the United States installed a vernacular tablet in the chapel. Sir Edwin, we read, obtained the Royal Assent (with danger and difficulty) to a constitution which was subsequently adopted in principle by many of the states of America. One of its wise provisions was that taxation should not be imposed without the consent of the taxed and it was, of course, non-observance of this taboo by the mother country one hundred and fifty years later that led to the American War of Independence. As a helpless victim of extortionate local rates and as the father of a son born in Virginia, I feel respect and admiration for Sir Edwin Sandys on both counts. It would, I think, be more beneficial for our prosperity today if his marble representation was hanging in the chapel of the House of Commons rather than languishing in the obscurity of a Norman church in a tiny hamlet in Kent. At least his memory has been preserved here for nearly four hundred years even if his principles are ignored elsewhere.

SUTTON BY DOVER
St. Peter and St. Paul

South farmstead

Coming after the relatively rare cruciform church at Northbourne, Sutton, smaller and altogether more modest, is an unexpected surprise, being the only apsidal country church that I can remember in Kent. The smi-circular end to the chancel that forms the feature of my drawing is Victorian, having been commissioned by Mr Maunday Harvey, the rector who did so much for this church during his incumbency. The recent advent of the apse is announced, I think, by the over-elaboration of the windows and by the connecting string course. In fact the apse is said to follow the original Norman plan for this church; 'by an earthquake happening 5th April 1580 a piece of this church fell down' and the present apse is the replacement. Fortunately nothing similar is recorded, so far as I know, for Northbourne although it is true that there are a couple of supplementary buttresses to the tower — earthquakes cannot be all that local, but perhaps it was just the merest tremor which disturbed Sutton on its hillside. Anyway, if the new apse looks unauthentic, it in no way detracts from the rugged simplicity of the Norman nave and chancel.

The other external change concerns the solitary bell. In the time of Maunday Harvey there was a small wooden belfry at the west end of the nave; now there is the shell of a blocked bell-cote and the bell is supported externally by a metal frame which is attached to the west face of the nave. The churchwarden, from whom I obtained the key, told me that the bell is of enormous age, cast in thirteen something as I remember, and one of the oldest in the country. The owner of the house below the church told me that a year or two ago it cost the parish some £300 to drill through the three foot thick wall for the bell's operating mechanism — only to be expected of a Norman wall.

Inside, one is greeted by three decorated Norman arches; the doorway arch, the chancel arch and the sanctuary arch. They all match, employing the same billet motif. The sanctuary arch appears to be in mint condition and must, I think, be a Victorian replica of what was originally there, so one could say it is Norman by intent and ancestry. The pews are boxed and the short range of choir stalls boasts dark, handsome, poppyhead finials to the bench ends. Around the inner circumference of the apse the Victorians arranged a pillared arcade, whose columns each bear different capitals. Quite clearly expense was not a matter of concern to the Rev. Maunday Harvey.

I suppose though that the most intriguing aspect of Sutton church is the pair of grotesque stone heads, one the keystone of the chancel arch, the other above the vestry window. As with all such primitive heads, which are crude and invariably convey a subtle air of menace, one cannot fail to be moved by faces that have stared down with unseeing eyes for century after century. One can well imagine the medieval peasants crossing themselves when they felt those basilisk eyes meeting theirs. The early fathers of the Church did not approve of like things and in 787 AD, at the Second Nicene Council, they roundly condemned as 'puerile and impious' these frivolous carvings. To judge by the number of faces one sees, little notice was taken of the edict in such a remote province of the Church as England.

The detached, black wooden belfry is what most people come to Brookland to see and rightly so; it is remarkable – a triple-tiered octagonal cone on a timber structure, the joinery of which encourages the experts to date it as 13th century or earlier. Its door was locked when I was there, but I could just make out the aged posts which must have come from trees growing a thousand years ago. There have been various fanciful attempts to explain why the bell tower follows Italian practice and sits beside the church, but I think the name gives it all away. There are watery ditches on at least two sides of the church and the foundations must be uncertain. This conclusion is corroborated inside the church where one can see that there is inadequate support even for the modest thrust of the arcade pillars. Both sides lean perilously outwards, one foot in fourteen feet of height. Between the arcades stretch tie beams which support the king posts for the roof; why these beams have not come down, if the opposing wall plates have separated by approximately two feet, is a mystery to me. Clearly they were wise to place the belfry on its own foundation.

To be honest, although the belfry may be the attraction here, I think the rugged old church can manage perfectly well on its own merits. Long and low, it was built about 1250 of a genial mishmash of rubble stones of varying sizes which have been allowed to mellow and age without the usual well-intentioned repointing. At present the church is appealing for £21,000 for restoration and there were men active on the roof, but with luck repointing will not figure on the current repair agenda.

The church's interior is most attractive – clean and bright with Georgian box pews of unpainted deal comfortably ensconced on an unrestored floor of quarry tiles. According to the admirable pamphlet, in medieval times these floor tiles cost all of a penny a hundred. Of the monuments, the most notable and substantial is the plain Bethersden marble chest tomb which, in solitary state in the south chapel, dates from 1615. Above it, recently revealed in 1964, is a fragment of a wall painting depicting the murder of Thomas Becket. One feels, not only for the archbishop whose intransigence roused the king's ire, but also for poor Grimm, his attendant chaplain, who would have been lucky to have escaped with his life, I suspect.

No doubt of greater historical significance than the detached belfry is Brookland's lead font. No account of the church fails to describe this cistern in great detail – here I will simply repeat the pamphlet and say that it is held to be the most important of the thirty lead fonts in this country. It is reputed to be 12th century, older than the church, and of French origin; one can only look on it with respect.

A last memory of Brookland that I shall retain with pleasure was the churchyard warning to 'BEWARE OF RAMS'.

FAIRFIELD
St. Thomas à Becket

Fair open land

This is an extraordinary little church. If one found it in a suburb or a new satellite town one might not give it a second glance, but planted where it is, absolutely in the middle of nowhere south of Appledore, hemmed in on all sides by water-filled ditches and with no tree or fence for protection or tombstone for remembrance and only sheep and wheeling seabirds for company, well, one can only wonder at what it is doing here.

Its relatively modern appearance of brick and tiles is genuine enough. Apparently there has been a church here since the early 1200s, but the original building was of timber frame and plaster. Before the marsh was properly dyked the church was liable to flood and in time the timbers rotted. This must have happened several times over the centuries and the church repaired more than once, as Hasted remarked when he came here in the late 1700s. The latest rescue was made in 1912 when the existing structure was dismantled and painstakingly re-erected, with the present brick fabric as an outer skin. It seems oddly other-worldly that this lonely simple little church should have received so much careful attention over the years; one could understand it had it been the shrine of some miracle, but there seems no particular reason for a church in the middle of a marsh to be so cossetted. We can only be grateful.

It is locked, of course, and the key kept at a local farm. It does not matter, for the low, rectangular leaded windows let one see the limited interior without difficulty. One might, if one did not know, expect to see a bare, cobwebby, unused nave and chancel; instead one finds the tiny spaces packed with 18th century church furniture — high white-painted box pews overlooked by a matching triple-decker pulpit and, in the miniature chancel, an altar surrounded by a banistered rail and, equally surprising, a vase of fresh flowers. It all looked spotless, quite charming and hardly to be believed. One is reminded of the timber framing by the equally spaced vertical studding posts in the plastered wall and by the low cross beam which gives the structure the appearance of a snug farmyard barn. The church possesses a famous font and that, too, one could see from the outside.

As I contemplated this diminutive church in the vast expanse of Walland Marsh, I could not help reflecting on the other 'lost' churches of the Marsh. It seems a paradox that primitive Fairfield, of lath and plaster and timber construction, should have outlasted solid stone, but of Hope All Saints and Midley all that remains are jagged stumps of wall and all that marks the sites of Fawkenhurst and Orgarswick are memorial crosses. They lost their villages, and congregations too no doubt; Fairfield has no village — I wonder if it ever had one — and its congregation must be scattered and sparse. So is it not redundant as one might expect? Enlightenment came when I crossed the marsh and gained the road. There, by the roadside opposite the suggestion of a causeway to the dyke-bound church, stands the church's notice board, on which I read that a service was to be held on one Sunday in May. That would explain the vase of flowers too.

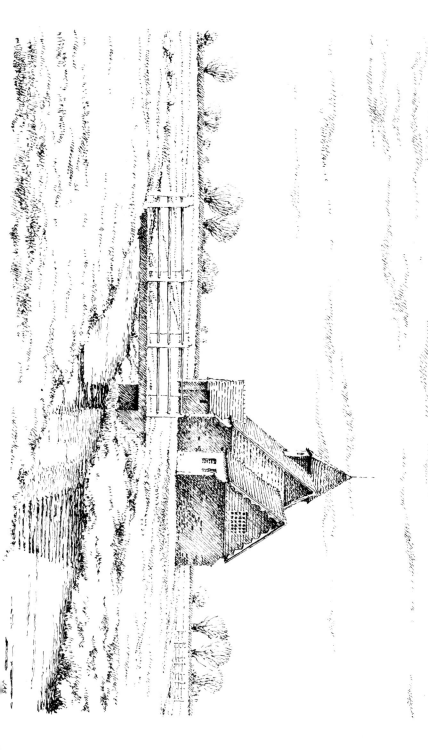

If Chislet church was near enough to the coast, as once it was, to figure on a nautical chart, it would be marked 'conspic'. Now its great bulk towers above the level Chislet marshes and is only rivalled scenically by the cooling towers of Richborough power station. One might be looking at a French chateau rather than a Norman church; it is, of course, the truncated spire that gives the gallic look. Close to, one forgets the continental comparison in favour of the antiquity of which that tower, with its crumbled rendering, flint and tile and rubble construction, and its bracings of metal clamps, speaks so eloquently. It is apparently one of only two in Kent that is central, but without transepts – the other being a ruin. Chislet is not a ruin; it is like some warrior of the past that has endured much and survived, but with the scars to show and it is all the more interesting for its topless tower.

The western nave seems contemporary and equally weather-beaten. From where I sat beside the yews that lead up to the church, I could clearly see in the gable end that there has been enlargement. Why should this be so, I wondered? Chislet is now barely an entity on the map and even if there were high hopes in 1918 when the short-lived coal mine was sunk nearby, the addition to the nave was made long before. There must be a reason hidden in history – perhaps connected with the monks of St. Augustine at Canterbury. The chancel is Early English, but looks altogether more modern and has evidently been receiving attention lately. The four doors to the church were all locked and looked unused; an impression of disuse that was confirmed by the bare, untidy aspect of the nave so far as I could make out through one of the north aisle windows. Unfortunately my restricted field of view could not command the chancel and the base of the tower where the unusual priest's chamber, as reported by Arthur Mee, must be. However, as is so often the case with cursory impressions, mine was wrong and I was informed across the churchyard wall that the church now doubles as a community centre – the chancel for religion, the nave and aisles for anything else of a worthy nature.

This modern version of medieval practice seems to have conferred a new lease of life on the church – more usage, repairs to the chancel, new tiles on the roof and a new central heating system, all within the last few years I was told. The new heating was so welcome (one can guess how cold it is here in January) that someone was provoked into painting 'Alleluia' on the new oil tank. Fortunately, and I hope by intent, all these improvements have not impaired the marvellous patina of old age that the walls and tower of this church exhibit. The oil tank may be 20th century but the tower is indubitably 12th century and looks it.

As I sat happily in the long grass surrounded by tombstones and the capstones of vaults half buried by thistles, cow parsley and the unidentifiable greenery of the countryside, I was delighted to watch an advance party of swifts performing their acrobatics about the churchyard. Summer had come to Chislet.

Bathed in the heady pungent aroma of cattle from the adjoining farmyard, Hoath church sits comfortably beside the road like a Victorian painting and Victorian is what, I suppose, it essentially now is. A straightforward nave, newly rendered in primrose stucco, with a shingled spire and a black and white porch, a chancel of large rough flints and a north aisle, also of flint, complete the external inventory. The aisle, the latest addition, despite its set of regular windows in their equal courses of close-set knapped flints, confuses. In its wall the Victorian architect has inserted the dripstone of an ancient doorway, perhaps to create an air of antiquity. Why should he do so – he could not hope to fool anyone, at least not for a couple of hundred years. Possibly there was a north doorway in the nave which became redundant when the aisle was added and he was reluctant to discard all trace of it.

Inside, the Victorian impression is faithfully preserved by the dark stained beams of the wagon roof and by the heavily and intricately carved reredos. The embroidered woollen hassocks may be modern, but they also have all the flavour of Victoriana for me. I was beginning to wonder what I was doing at Hoath when my eye landed on the ledger stone, dated 1803 and Georgian for a change, and beside it the head-less brass which Pevsner dates as c.1430. At last, out of the 19th century and back to the days of the warring houses of York and Lancaster. I do not know when they stopped using carved heads as corbels, but this little church has three – two as much worn down stops to the doorway drip stone in the porch, and a third, difficult to make out, high on the east wall above the reredos. These heads would surely antedate the brass on the floor below the chancel but, nevertheless, it is the brass that must be the cherished possession here. Later on I did to my satisfaction identify two shadows of scratch dials on the south western corner of the nave. These could possibly be the earliest datable items of a church from which the past has been virtually restored out of existence, but which they say was laid down in 1303, only four years after the signing of the Magna Carta.

On the east side of the neat churchyard, balancing the aromatic farmyard, is that other accessory of a country church, the pub. Hoath's is called the Admiral Rodney and, having entered the Navy in 1935 by way of the Rodney Term at Dartmouth, I was only too ready to have my beer and sandwiches under his banner. It is always a mystery to me why there are so many pubs in honour of the Marquis of Granby, who fought the French at Minden, and so few to Rodney who fought the French at sea and who no less deserved the gratitude of his country. It is not a grand pub and the admiral would be disappointed, I fear, but with his name so overlooked, one should not be choosy; at any rate I was grateful that my explor-ation and sketch of this relatively ordinary little church, chapel that was, at Hoath should have provided me with a reminder of my old hero and awakened memories of my departed youth.

There are two churches at Hawkhurst, the one you see beside the road to Rye, the other a mile to the south beyond the village green. This is the one I have drawn. What possessed the authorities to commission Sir George Gilbert Scott to design a second church in 1860 is beyond my comprehension when they already had a magnificent Perpendicular building no more than a step down the road.

St. Lawrence, the older partner, has more than enough of good things for two; battlemented north and south aisles, an array of windows that originated in 1350, a sturdy, confident west tower and north and south storied porches, also embattled. The north porch, that in use and facing the green, is decorated with painted bosses on the wooden ceiling, ledger stones on the floor and an elegant bench seat that would not disgrace a drawing room. The only criticism might refer to the room above where the headroom must be uncomfortably restricted. The south porch, no longer used, is vaulted with stone bosses of carved foliage — it seems too elaborate to languish unused but one can only go in one door at a time. Around the church stand ranks of grey, lichened tombstones. They range from 1633 and, as a foreground, they provide a more than usually agreeable contrast to the honey-coloured sandstone of the church. Sadly, today we seem to have lost the art of making such aesthetically satisfying memorials.

The church is as grand inside as it is impressive outside. The many windows are largely unstained and the whole effect is light, airy and uncluttered. Apparently a flying bomb fell in the churchyard in the last war and 'did considerable damage' with the result that most of the glass in the windows is new; if it was not for a splinter of twisted metal on one of the sills, one would never have suspected war damage here. Bombs apart, though, this church makes more effort than most to remember the war casualties and its north chapel, reputedly the earliest part and now christened the 'Warrior Chapel', contains the names of the fallen in both world wars. It always seems churlish to me that the Boer, Crimean and Napoleonic wars were not similarly commemorated but perhaps wars in those days did not affect the whole population as profoundly as they have in the 20th century.

I scoured the inside of the church and scrutinised every inscription but nowhere could I find the memorial I was seeking — that to the astronomer John Herschel. It seemed inconceivable that the most famous resident of Hawkhurst should be ignored in his village church and I am afraid that I distracted a flower-arranger who was put out by her inability to remember where he lay, particularly as he had apparently figured prominently in a local pageant a year ago. Eventually we gave it up and it was only when I was on my way home that I guessed where he might be — Westminster Abbey, beside Sir Isaac Newton. I read later that one of the south windows celebrated his exploration of the heavens. Perhaps it was one of those damaged by the bomb; not the sort of treatment for a savant of German extraction to suffer from a fellow countryman.

Benenden and Hawkhurst churches seem almost identical — if they swopped places I wonder who would know the difference? They are both of sandstone, streaked with iron, with embattled north and south porches and much the same sort of west tower with its clock on the north face. Benenden's construction history is the more turbulent and varied although it takes an expert to recognise the changes; it looked all of a piece to me and just as fine as Hawkhurst. Both speak of the wealden wealth that accrued from the iron industry of the Middle Ages when this part of Kent provided cannon for the king and nails for his horses.

Apparently in 1672 the church was 'ruined by storm'; that is to say the roof and woodwork were consumed by fire, as was the detached wooden belfry. This stood 132 feet high — all gone in the space of five hours. How often does one read of churches almost destroyed by fire and one can well understand the difficulty, impossibility in those days even, of putting out the flames when the roof timbers were well alight. Rebuilding was immediate and thorough; the hybrid 13th, 14th and 15th century remained but the pillars that support the roof were replaced and a new tower was incorporated at the west end of the nave. It stands sixty feet high and dominates as a tower should. Imagine what the wooden belfry, nearly twice the height, must have looked like. With it Benenden overshadowed Brookland, now the sole representative of the campanile style in Kent. Rebuilding took no more than two years and some may have thought that the work was rushed. One at least, the Victorian squire, the Earl of Cranbrook, was apparently dissatisfied so in 1861 the arcade pillars and roof supports were renewed at his expense. Much else was altered, but whether it has all been improved one cannot tell and I rather doubt it. However it remains a very fine church, inside and out, and still receives the attention it deserves if the scaffolding around the chancel is anything to go by.

Benenden's most historic personage, or at any rate he who has the most imposing monument, is Admiral of the Fleet Sir John Norris. He served in the Navy at a time when war seemed almost endemic and he rose to be the Commander-in-Chief of the Channel Fleet in the Seven Years War when the French were contemplating invasion. A timely gale dispersed the assembling French and the admiral was deprived of the opportunity to add to his laurels and join the ranks of the great sea victors. The inscription on his monument in the south chapel does not mention, very correctly, that he was known in the Navy as 'Foulweather Jack'.

Benenden village is now, I suppose, as much renowned for the girls' school as it is for the medieval church and presumably the congregation is suitably fortified every Sunday. I wonder how many of those impressionable girls look up, as they troop in through the north porch, to admire the carved salamander boss that holds the vaulted porch together. My dictionary defines a salamander as a 'lizard-like animal supposed to live in fire'; a fitting symbol for a church successfully rescued from the ashes of a destructive fire.

Just to show that one is not entirely obsessed with medieval churches to the exclusion of all others, here is one Victorian church to prove it, and a worthy representative it is. Not to put too fine a point on it, this little church, built by the Beresfords in the 1840s, is an absolute gem. To eulogise a bit, Kilndown is to other churches as a Fabergé trinket is to other objets d'art.

In plan it is rather like Mereworth church, a simple rectangle with a stone steeple at the west end through which one enters. Mereworth is Christopher Wren baroque whereas Kilndown is Pre-Raphaelite Gothic Revival, if I may be permitted such an opinionated distinction, so the two are similar yet unlike. Externally, Kilndown looks very well, not too new and not too fussily Victorian – but how many country churches have a stone, vaulted lych-gate, or once had a churchyard mausoleum copied from the Scaglia family tomb at Verona? This is where the founder, Viscount Beresford (one of Wellington's generals) lies along with others of his family. In the 1920s the elaborate canopy above his tomb was taken down as unsafe; I cannot imagine that the Field Marshal would have countenanced that liberty, or that it would be accepted today when we are more conscious of our responsibilities to the past and to the future.

However it is the inside that rivets at Kilndown and is what made this remote country church in a tiny Kent hamlet a model for Victorian church interiors. Every last thing seems to have received careful design and immaculate execution in accordance with one unifying theme and one overall colour scheme. The theme is Gothic and the colours red, blue and gold. Take, for instance, the inner doors, all uniform and carved to represent a Gothic facade of pinnacles and vertical moulding; take the font and pulpit, both carved and elaborate and painted throughout in red, blue and gold. The pulpit is based, so it is said, on a pulpit at Beaulieu Abbey. Placed high on the wall, it looks Italian and it needed a special external stair turret for concealed access. Take the poppy heads at the ends of the pews – all the same and yet each different in detail. Apart from the general air of quality, the supreme attainment is the screen stretching across the nave to create a shallow multi-coloured sanctuary. Whoever carved this screen must have gained enormous pleasure and satisfaction from his labour – Gothic again, intricate and transparent and decked in the tricolour livery. Splendid it is in a splendid interior.

One could go on rhapsodising about this church. My exploration was most thorough for I was joined by a villager who, I gathered, has made it his business to act as a sort of honorary custodian and handyman. It was from him that I learnt of the many changes, with a loss of character in some cases, that have taken place since Alexander Beresford Hope set himself the task of embellishing his stepfather's foundation. Between them they left a brilliant monument in this corner of Kent – one that any family would count an honour to claim, so it was rather disconcerting to learn from my informant that there are no Beresfords left here today to bask in its reflected glory.

HARTY
St. Thomas

In the same way that the church of St Thomas marks the end of the road in Sheppey, so, as the remotest church in Kent, it acts as an appropriate full stop to this volume of sketches. Overlooking the Swale estuary and separated from mainland Sheppey by two miles of marshy grazing, the church keeps company with two farm cottages, a bungalow that was a school and a derelict farmstead that looked to my inexperienced eye as if it has been converted into a grain store.

Prudently I took care to make my descent here on a Sunday and, although I found no service, they told me at the cottages that the church is always opened on Sundays. Inside I was greeted by that distinctive odour of damp, which is the incense of country churches, and by vases of spring flowers. This is a small church, twenty six yards long and fifteen wide, roughly paced, consisting of a nave, north aisle and chancel with unmatching north and south chapels, all diminutive. It is old, of course; the arcade of rectangular piers was cut in 1200 or so from the pre-existing Norman north wall, but the whole is good for several hundred years yet as the grey rubble-stone walling has obviously been repointed in the not too distant past.

Much as aspiring country houses covet an association with Elizabeth I, so self-respecting churches welcome the approval of Sir John Betjeman and he is quoted here with satisfaction by the church leaflet. It is the 'splendid isolation' by which he remembers Harty but I am sure that he would have seen, or been shown with pride, the early 15th century oak muniment chest — 'found floating in the Swale'. I would be surprised if he did not also remember the 14th century rood screens and the exposed, skeletal oak framework at the west end of the nave that underpins the bellcote. The frame seems more than adequate for the task but in fact it is reinforced externally by a central buttress. One would not have thought that so much support was necessary for stability were it not for the watery ditches on two sides of the churchyard, remnants of an earlier moat, suggesting that the water table cannot be far below the surface. This is not entirely improbable when one recalls that this particular part of Sheppey is more properly known as the Isle of Harty — which presumably it was before the marshes were dyked.

At the end of this odyssey in Kent, after exploring the hundred churches illustrated in my first little book and the second hundred in this, I am still as mystified as ever by the magic they exert. Here at Harty the cottages and the farm buildings could go and no-one would miss them, but not the irreplaceable little church. When these medieval churches were built they eclipsed all other buildings in the village in terms of size and quality. Now eight hundred years later, they still transcend in quality. It is a salutary thought that, if only one building in a village could be retained, most people I am sure would favour the church, and not just on grounds of antiquity. Why this feeling? Is it religious, aesthetic, historic or a combination of all three? Or is it a dimly felt recognition of the comfort these churches must have given to generations of our forbears through all those centuries? I am inclined to the last.